THE IDIOM BOOK

1010

American English Idioms
in
101 Two-Page Lessons

by
Hal Niergarth
with
Elizabeth Niergarth

PR LINGUA
LEARNING

Pro Lingua Learning

PO Box 4467

Rockville, MD 20849 USA

Office: 301-424-8900

Orders: 800-888-4741

Email: info@ProLinguaLearning.com

Web: www.ProLinguaLearning.com

At Pro Lingua
our objective is to foster an approach
to learning and teaching that we call
***interplay**, the **inter**action of language*
learners and teachers with their materials,
with the language and culture,
and with each other in active, creative,
*and productive **play**.*

Copyright © 2007, 2019 Hal Niergarth. My thanks to: Anne, Eric, and Laura

ISBN 978-0-86647-259-3

All rights reserved. This publication may not be reproduced or transmitted in any form or by any means, electronic, mechanical, photocopying, recording or other, or stored in an information storage or retrieval system without permission in writing from the publisher. However, permission to copy is granted by the publisher as follows:

TEACHERS MAY COPY INDIVIDUAL LESSONS FOR CLASSROOM USE ONLY

Contents

Introduction	1	
1 Concert	2	
2 Car Mechanic	4	
3 Dormitory Life	6	
4 Transition	8	
5 Roommates	10	
6 New Job	12	
7 Check-up	14	
8 Wedding Reception	16	
9 Public Transport	18	
10 Airport Arrival	20	
11 Getting There is Half the Fun	22	
12 Careless Driver	24	
13 Editor's Office	26	
14 On the Job	28	
15 Family	30	
16 Exercise	32	
17 A Chilly Romance	34	
18 Local Cuisine	36	
19 Job Interview	38	
20 Cutting Corners	40	
21 Hiking	42	
22 Used Car	44	
23 Spring	46	
24 New Apartment	48	
25 Visit to the Doctor	50	
26 Bad Dog	52	
27 Shakespeare Festival	54	
28 Possible Business Merger	56	
29 Big Guns	58	
30 Car Repair	60	
31 House Maintenance	62	
32 A Job in Toronto	64	
33 Long Time No See	66	
34 Technical Training	68	
35 Roughing It	70	
36 The English Language	72	
37 Field Botany	74	
38 Taking a Chance on Love	76	
39 Praise & Thanks	78	
40 East Michigan to Massachusetts	80	
41 Neighbors	82	
42 Management Differences	84	
43 ESL	86	
44 Exercise	88	
45 Politics	90	
46 Downsized	92	
47 Bashful Boy	94	
48 Basic Training	96	
49 Rock Climbing	98	
50 Basketball Win	100	
51 At the Cottage	102	

#	Title	Page
52	National Leaders	104
53	Talk Show	106
54	Traveling	108
55	Flying First Class	110
56	Energy Crisis	112
57	The Winning Ticket	114
58	Face to Face	116
59	Commuting	118
60	Organic or Processed?	120
61	Advice	122
62	Reunion	124
63	In Training at the Factory	126
64	Sales Meeting	128
65	Snow and Final Exams	130
66	Diplomacy	132
67	Winter Fun	134
68	Dirty Tricks	136
69	Who's Paying?	138
70	College Dorms	140
71	Academic Advice	142
72	Breaking the News	144
73	Speeding Ticket	146
74	Lucky?	148
75	More Therapy	150
76	At the Ledges	152
77	More Heat than Light	154
78	Big Mouth	156
79	Mending Fences	158
80	Trip to the Beach	160
81	Forever Young?	162
82	Risky Business	164
83	Cabin Fever	166
84	Furnished Apartment	168
85	Election	170
86	Uncle Ralph	172
87	Table Manners	174
88	Office Squabble	176
89	Dirty Windows	178
90	Expired License	180
91	Lexicography	182
92	The Latest Big Thing	184
93	Investment Opportunity	186
94	Keep Your Shirt On	188
95	Death and Taxes	190
96	Stormy Weather	192
97	Bank Loan	194
98	Company Profits	196
99	Setting up Shop	198
100	Demotion	200
101	Sooner or Later	202

Other Books from Pro Lingua
for Intermediate/Advanced
Learners   204

Introduction

This book was written for *high-intermediate/advanced* learners of English. The topical content is suitable for *young adults and adults*. The language used in the lessons is very colloquial, intended to represent the linguistic expression of native speakers interacting socially in informal personal and professional contexts.

Each lesson features 10 idioms with emphasis on expressions that naturally occur in idiomatic discourse. As such, many of these idiomatic expressions are logical connectors that hold spoken and informal written discourse together.

The book is divided into 101 lessons, and each lesson has four sections on two facing pages.

Section A. The idioms are introduced in the context of an *idiomatic conversation*. Most of the conversations are informal and many are conversations between close friends or family members. These conversations are available on two CDs.

Section B. The same ten idioms are presented in a different format. Most of them are in the form of *written messages*. The idioms are gapped, requiring the learner to pay attention to the form of the idiom, referring to section A if necessary. The messages include emails, journal entries, notes, and memos. The language is informal.

Section C. This *matching exercise* increases the learning challenge. The idioms in the left column are matched with an entry in the right column that defines or otherwise gives meaning to the idiom. Note that the 10 entries are broken into two groups. The first four idioms and their meanings are the first group, and the last six form another group. The exercise is broken to keep the activity from being overwhelming. Brackets are used occasionally to provide explanation.

Section D. The learners are asked to *use the idioms by writing a sentence* in which they are substituting one of the idioms for an equivalent non-idiomatic phrase or sentence. The ten sentences follow the order in which the idioms are presented in Section A. Therefore, the learner working on sentence number one can refer to Section A and find the idiom that should be used to paraphrase the phrasing in sentence number one.

The answers to sections C and D are available on the Pro Lingua web site, along with a complete list of the idioms. www.ProLinguaAssociates.com

Lesson 1

CONCERT

1A. Read.

Luis: <u>What do you say</u> we go to the concert tonight?

Carlos: Well, <u>at the moment</u>, I don't have any money.

Luis: It only costs ten bucks to get in. The drinks are what cost you <u>an arm and a leg</u>.

Carlos: I don't know if I'<u>m up to</u> facing hundreds of drunken college students.

Luis: Man, you really are <u>in a</u> real <u>funk</u>, aren't you?

Carlos: Well, I've <u>been broke</u> for a long time, and I still don't <u>see light at the end of the tunnel</u>.

Luis: Come on! It'll do you good to <u>get your mind off</u> your troubles.

Carlos: <u>What the hell</u>, why not.

Luis: And I'll <u>pick up the tab</u>.

Carlos: The way I feel, I hope you have a lot of money.

1B. Read and fill in the blanks.

Subject: Money
Date: Saturday, March 24
From: Carlos Gomez <cgomez @ supersend.net>
To: Pedro Gomez <Pedrog@ novanet.com>

Dear Pedro,

How are you? I'm OK, but <u>at the moment</u> I'm <u>in a</u> _____, and I <u>am</u> _____ because of a big concert that I went to last night. The admission was only ten bucks, but I had to pay <u>an</u> _____ <u>and a leg</u> for drinks that I bought for a girl I met there. Then I played poker after, and lost a lot of money. I can't pay my rent and I'm behind in my school work, and right now I'm unable to do any serious studying. I can't <u>see any light at the end of the</u> _____, so <u>are</u> you ____ <u>to</u> lending me a few hundred? <u>What do</u> _____ <u>say</u>? It would sure <u>get my</u> _____ <u>off</u> my problems if you could help me. If you can meet me down at the Blue Eagle Cafe with the money, I'll even _____ <u>up the tab</u> for our lunch (with your dough, of course)! But if I do get evicted, <u>what</u> _____ <u>hell</u>: I'll survive.

Love to Mama and Papa.

Carlos

2   The Idiom Book

1C. Matching Exercise. In the parentheses write the letter of the meaning for each idiom.

Idiom

1) what do you say (c)
2) be up to ( )
3) an arm and a leg ( )
4) at the moment ( )
5) see light at the end of the tunnel (j)
6) be broke ( )
7) in a funk ( )
8) get your mind off your troubles ( )
9) pick up the tab ( )
10) what the hell ( )

Meaning

(a) ready and able to do something
(b) a lot of money
(c) (1) I suggest that. . . . (2) What's your answer?
(d) right now
(e) to forget about one's problems
(f) to pay someone else's bill
(g) I don't care
(h) have no money
(i) a sad or dejected state
(j) to see or know that something bad, or unpleasant is ending.

1D. Change each of the following sentences with an idiom from 1C.

1) <u>I suggest that</u> we go for a swim. <u>What do you say we go for a swim.</u>
2) Right now I'm pretty busy. _____
3) My new computer cost me a lot of money. _____
4) I don't feel like climbing that hill. _____
5) Since his fight with Yuko he's been really sad and dejected. _____
6) I'm really without any money! _____
7) She's had health and money problems for a long time and still doesn't know if or when they'll end. _____
8) Come on to the party with us; it'll help you forget your problems. _____
9) I don't care. I'll try it. _____
10) We'll pay your bill. _____

The Idiom Book 3

Lesson 2

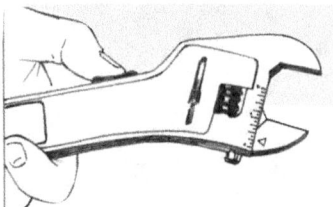

CAR MECHANIC

2A. Read.

Hal: Morning Pete; Hal here. My brakes don't work as well as they <u>used to</u>.

Pete: And you don't want to <u>meet your maker</u> in a fiery freeway crash because that so-called mechanic that you <u>go to</u> doesn't <u>know his stuff</u>, eh?

Hal: OK. <u>I've seen the light</u>. I'd have to <u>have a screw loose</u> to patronize him again. The last time I was there he <u>set fire to</u> his pants with a cutting torch.

Pete: I can <u>put my finger on</u> the main cause of your brake problem right now: that guy's stupid.

Hal: People that incompetent are, luckily, <u>few and far between</u>. I think I'll come back to you; you're expensive, but you're also a <u>straight shooter.</u>

2B. Read and fill in the blanks.

Journal Entry for 3/25

Our neighbor, the director of a medical clinic I ____ to <u>go</u>____, <u>met her</u>_____ last week. She really _____ <u>her stuff</u> when it came to diagnosis. Sometimes she could <u>put her</u> _____ <u>on</u> a condition just by looking at my complexion and especially at my eyes. She did <u>have a few screws</u> _____: once she threw kerosene on a charcoal barbecue she was tending and ____<u>fire to</u> her wig. After I teased her for about an hour she ____ <u>the light</u> and agreed to buy a gas-fired barbecue. She was a _____ <u>shooter</u> and a warm friend. People like her are <u>few</u>____ <u>far between</u>.

4 The Idiom Book

2C. Matching Exercise. In the parentheses write the letter of the meaning for each idiom.

Idiom

1) go to (　)
2) used to (　)
3) meet one's maker (　)
4) know one's stuff (　)
5) few and far between (　)
6) have (got) a screw loose (　)
7) straight shooter (　)
8) see the light (　)
9) set fire to (　)
10) put one's finger on (　)

Meaning

(a) to be competent and efficient
(b) to die
(c) to visit or patronize regularly
(d) did habitually in the past
(e) to understand
(f) an honest person
(g) rare; uncommon
(h) to make something start to burn
(i) to be eccentric, or a little crazy
(j) to assess or perceive correctly

2D. Change each of the following sentences with an idiom from 2C.

1) I once worked in New York City. _____

2) Old Uncle Fudd died last week. _____

3) My boyfriend visits a chiropractor for a back problem. _____

4) My sister's a computer technician; she's really good at her job. _____

5) I told my brother he'd have to work hard in college. At last he understood and began to study hard. _____

6) My neighbor talks to his tomato plants. He's very strange. _____

7) The children who burned the garage down were playing with matches. _____

8) That mechanic can usually spot the problem's cause in five minutes. _____

9) Honest politicians are pretty rare in this country. _____

10) We urgently need an honest, intelligent person for our national leader. _____

Lesson 3

DORMITORY LIFE

3A. Read.

Roger: Last night I couldn't study <u>at all</u>.

Jack: Let me guess. Your loudmouth roommate couldn't stop talking.

Roger: Jack, <u>what's with</u> that loudmouth, anyway? He's a real <u>pain in the butt</u>.

Jack: I'm guessing he was <u>hot stuff</u> in high school and <u>threw his weight around</u> there. Kids like that always seem to have the habit of <u>running off at the mouth</u>.

Roger: Dorm life here might get to be <u>a bit much</u>.

Jack: Yeah. I haven't <u>made up my mind</u> whether I'll stay here or look for a furnished room in town.

Roger: Well, a room <u>of your own</u> would be <u>a damn sight</u> quieter.

3B. Read and fill in the blanks.

My dear Gisela,

I've heard nothing <u>at</u>____ from you for two weeks. <u>What's</u>____ us? Please write or call.

Anyway, my new boss is a real _____ <u>in the butt</u>. He seems quite insecure and actually shouts out orders, apparently to let everyone know that he's ____ <u>stuff</u> and <u>throws his</u> _____ <u>around</u>. And he's always <u>running</u> _____ <u>at the mouth</u> and saying nothing. It's pitiful; I haven't <u>made up my</u> _____ whether to stay or look for a new job.

This place is getting to be <u>a bit</u> _____; I'd sure like to have a small business <u>of my</u> _____.

And I'd feel <u>a damn</u> _____ better if I heard from you.

Love always,

Your Roger

6 The Idiom Book

3C. Matching Exercise. In the parentheses write the letter of the meaning for each idiom.

Idiom

1) what's with (   )
2) hot stuff (   )
3) pain in the butt [coarse] (   )
4) at all (   )
5) a bit much (   )
6) run off at the mouth (   )
7) make up one's mind (   )
8) throw one's weight around (   )
9) of one's own (   )
10) a damn sight [informal] (   )

Meaning

(a) an important person
(b) an annoying person or thing
(c) completely, totally
(d) tell me about, or explain
(e) almost too [much]
(f) belonging to no one else
(g) a lot; much (in extent or degree)
(h) to decide
(i) to talk too much
(j) to act like the boss

3D. Change each of the following sentences with an idiom from 3C.

1) I really don't like broccoli! _____
2) Why does she look so sad? What's happened to her? _____
3) That guy's a nuisance: he always wants to borrow tools from me. _____
4) She walks around campus like she's really important. _____
5) My three-year-old sister runs things in our house. _____
6) My brother-in-law loves to talk a lot about things he knows nothing about. _____
7) The politician's "sincerity" was a little overdone. _____
8) She's finding it hard to decide about that job offer. _____
9) I'd sure like a bedroom that was mine alone. _____
10. With the new paint job, it looks a lot better than it did. _____

Lesson 4
TRANSITION

4A. Read.

Pat: We have to do some fairly careful scheduling, <u>what with</u> the move from Michigan to Massachusetts pending, the new job in Detroit starting in two weeks, my having to get Cookie's car from here to Massachusetts, and the little matter of finishing my book.

Peg: <u>Not to mention</u> your appointments with the doctor.

Pat: Well, those are <u>kind of</u> <u>up in the air</u> right now.

Peg: No! You can't just <u>put</u> them <u>on the back burner</u>. They're too important.

Pat: Hmm. Maybe you're right <u>at that</u>. I'll have to find time for them.

Peg: <u>For the life of me</u>, I don't know how we'll do it.

Pat: We'll get it done, <u>by hook or by crook</u>.

Peg: <u>What about</u> Detroit? A furnished room or a small apartment?

Pat: Something comfortable. <u>Within reason</u>, of course.

4B. Read and fill in the blanks.

Journal for 3/27

<u>What</u> _____ all the changes happening, we'll have a lot of important decisions to make. Damn—I've got simultaneous obligations to family and to the new job, <u>not to</u> _____ the publisher. The situation with the potential new landlord is ___<u>in the air</u>, and my car is <u>kind</u> ___ old for me to be putting much more money into it. And <u>what</u> _____ transport? I can't <u>put</u> any of these matters ___ <u>the back burner</u>, because they all need attention five minutes ago. <u>For the</u> _____ <u>of me</u>, I wonder that I stay so calm and good-natured. By God, I think I can do it, <u>at</u> _____. <u>By</u> _____ <u>or by crook</u>, I'll have to make an investment in another car, but _____ <u>reason</u>.

8 The Idiom Book

4C. Matching Exercise. In the parentheses write the letter of the meaning for each idiom.

Idiom

1) what with ( )
2) up in the air ( )
3) kind of ( )
4) not to mention ( )
5) at that ( )
6) put something on the back burner ( )
7) for the life of me ( )
8) what about ( )
9) within reason ( )
10) by hook or by crook ( )

Meaning

(a) not decided; uncertain
(b) to some degree; somewhat
(c) and of course
(d) because of
(e) despite everything;
(f) by any means necessary
(g) not excessive; reasonable
(h) Honestly! Truly!
(i) to postpone something
(j) and there's the issue (or question) of. . . .

4D. Change each of the following sentences with an idiom from 4C.

1) Because of everything happening right now, I'll have to call you back. _____

2) She's bright, funny, sweet, and of course beautiful. _____

3) I'm rather hungry. Could we eat now? _____
4) Our plan to go to China is still unsettled. _____
5) She had to postpone the decision about going to China. _____

6) Despite all that hassle I think I'll be able to complete the job on time. _____

7) Honestly, I don't know how you can work in this madhouse all day. _____

8) They're going to get to Hawaii any way that they can. _____

9) And there's the issue of Detroit. _____
10) I'd like to get an apartment that is inexpensive but not too small, of course. _____

The Idiom Book 9

Lesson 5

ROOMMATES

5A. Read.

Roger: <u>Let's face it</u>: the food in this dorm just doesn't <u>cut it</u>.

Joe: So, <u>why don't</u> we get a little fridge in here and at least fix our own breakfast every morning.

Roger: There are <u>any number</u> of reasons why that's a bad idea. <u>For one thing</u>, it'd be unsanitary. For another, I know I'd get <u>stuck with</u> all the clean-up work.

Joe: No, no. <u>So help me</u>, I'd do my share. <u>In fact</u>, I'd <u>do the dishes</u> every morning.

Roger: OK, OK, <u>I'm willing to</u> give it a try.

5B. Read and fill in the blanks.

Joe:

    <u>Let's</u> ____ it: the division of labor we arranged just doesn't <u>cut</u> ____ for <u>any</u> _____ of reasons. <u>For one</u> _____, I'm always _____ with _____ the dishes. ____ fact, you've never done them even once. <u>So</u> _____ me, I've tried to make it work, and I guess you have too, in your own way. I said I <u>was</u> _____ to try, but now I know that we're just not suited to be roommates, so <u>why</u> _____ we end it now, amicably.

Roger

P.S. I'll be back tomorrow. Let's talk.

5C. Matching Exercise. In the parentheses write the letter of the meaning for each idiom.

Idiom

1) why don't ( )
2) let's face it ( )
3) cut it ( )
4) any number ( )
5) so help me ( )
6) stuck with ( )
7) do the dishes ( )
8) in fact ( )
9) for one thing ( )
10) be willing to ( )

Meaning

(a) a lot
(b) I suggest that. . . .
(c) to be satisfactory, or good enough
(d) this is a regrettable truth:
(e) truly
(f) to wash all the utensils and containers used for a meal
(g) to agree to do something
(h) I swear that this is the truth:
(i) forced to do something disagreeable
(j) here is one reason:

5D. Change each of the following sentences with an idiom from 5A.

1) This is the unfortunate truth: your academic work is poor. _____

2) I'm afraid this essay isn't good enough. _____
3) I suggest that you use the student tutoring service. _____

4) You often make a lot of spelling errors. _____
5) Here is one reason: You don't read English-language newspapers. _____

6) And now I've been asked to give you this bad news. _____

7) This is really the truth: I've been trying hard to help you and not discourage you. _____

8) Truly, I've overlooked a lot of your mistakes. _____
9) Maybe you and your roomie could hold spelling contests while you're washing the breakfast things. _____

10) If you agree to do that, it might help. _____

The Idiom Book

Lesson 6

NEW JOB

6A. Read.

Al: Guess what! I've got a new job. The guy <u>next door</u> is a <u>big shot</u> at the factory, and he told me about the opening.

Zeke: Did he say he'd <u>put in a good word for</u> you?

Al: <u>Not in so many words</u>, but he <u>sort of</u> hinted at it.

Zeke: Anyway—<u>nice going</u>. I know you'll <u>make your mark</u> there.

Al: Say, since you have <u>all sorts of</u> time, and we have all sorts of goodies here, <u>how about</u> a coffee and a doughnut?

Zeke: Well, we shouldn't let them <u>go to waste</u>.

6B. Read and fill in the blanks.

> To: Bob Johnson <bobj@swiftnet.com>
> Cc:
> Subject: Job for you?
> Attachments: *none*
>
> Hey Bob,
>
>   We live _____<u>door to</u> a woman who's a ____<u>shot</u> at Inkwell Publishing. She was here last night for dinner. She told me they're looking for a good foreign editor and I <u>put in a good</u> _____ for you. She ____ of indicated—<u>not in so</u> _____ words but by hinting—that she'd like to talk to you about the job. Incidentally, _____<u>going</u> on that article about East Asia's energy situation. I'm sure that you'll <u>make your</u> _____ with Inkwell if you go there.
>   You know, we have <u>all</u> _____ of left-over goodies here, so ____<u>about</u> coming over tonight? We don't want this to __<u>to waste</u>.
>
>   Art and Martha

6C. Matching Exercise. In the parentheses, write the letter of the meaning for each idiom.

Idiom

1) in so many words ( )
2) next door [to] ( )
3) put in a good word for someone ( )
4) big shot ( )
5) all sorts of ( )
6) how about ( )
7) make one's mark ( )
8) sort of ( )
9) go to waste ( )
10) nice going ( )

Meaning

(a) clearly, directly, and literally
(b) to say something complimentary about someone
(c) an important person
(d) in the dwelling or building beside someone
(e) a lot of
(f) Would you like. . . .
(g) not be used, drunk, or eaten; be wasted
(h) become successful or famous
(i) congratulations
(j) somewhat; rather

6D. Change each of the following sentences with an idiom from 6C.

1) My sister lives in the house right beside ours. _____

2) His wife is a vice president at company headquarters. _____

3) Please say something complimentary about me to the coach. _____

4) He hasn't told me plainly, clearly, and literally, but I know he loves me. _____

5) The news rather disappointed me. _____

6) Congratulations. You did a good job. _____

7) With her talent, she'll become famous as a writer. _____

8) He always has lots of excuses for being late. _____

9) Would you like. . . . _____

10) The food for the picnic didn't get eaten. _____

Lesson 7

CHECK-UP

7A. Read.

Andy: Doc, I don't feel <u>so hot</u> <u>these days</u>.

Dr: Hmm. Let me <u>take a look at</u> your vitals while you tell me what you've been <u>up to</u> lately.

Andy: Well, I've been <u>working my butt off</u>; I'm <u>up for</u> a promotion and I don't want to <u>blow it</u>.

Dr: If you're up for it, that probably means that they think you <u>have it coming</u>, so just relax and let it happen.

Andy: <u>Easier said than done</u>.

Dr: <u>Take it easy</u>. You'll get the promotion.

7B. Read and fill in the blanks.

Journal 4/15

Things aren't going <u>so</u>____ for the business _____<u>days</u>. If you <u>take a look</u>____ the balance sheet, you'll see what we've <u>been up</u>____: <u>working our</u> _____ off with almost no results. I'm <u>up</u>____ a promotion but I know I'll <u>blow</u>____ if business doesn't improve. I feel I ____ <u>it coming</u>, but getting it is <u>easier</u> _____ <u>than done</u>. I'd sure like to be able to <u>take</u> ____ <u>easy</u> for a change.

7C. Matching Exercise. In the parentheses, write the letter of the meaning for each idiom.

Idiom

1) (not) so hot ( )
2) be up to ( )
3) take a look at ( )
4) these days ( )
5) take it easy ( )
6) up for ( )
7) blow it ( )
8) have it coming ( )
9) easier said than done ( )
10) work my butt off ( )

Meaning

(a) engaged in; busy with; doing
(b) inspect; examine
(c) currently; now
(d) not very good
(e) to deserve something
(f) easy to talk about but hard to do
(g) to relax and rest; not be upset
(h) to spoil or ruin something; fail
(i) eligible and being considered for something
(j) to work very hard

7D. Change the following sentences with an idiom from 7C.

1) How do you feel Honey? You don't look very good. _____

2) Hi Sanjay. What are you busy with nowadays? [Two idioms] _____

3) I want to inspect that contract again. _____

4) I've worked really hard on this project. _____

5) I'm eligible for that promotion, and they're considering me. _____

6) I have a crack at that new job and I'm not going to ruin my chance. _____

7) I deserve the promotion. _____

8) It's easy to talk about making money, but it's pretty hard to actually do it. _____

9) It would be nice to get some rest and relaxation for a while. _____

The Idiom Book **15**

Lesson 8
WEDDING RECEPTION

8A. Read.

Martin: I went to Anya and Kolya's reception. It was one <u>hell of a</u> party.

Brenda: Was it a <u>mob scene</u>?

Martin: There were <u>a good</u> 300 people there.

Brenda: <u>How about</u> the band. Was it any good?

Martin: It sure was. And when it first <u>struck up</u>, Kolya went out and did a kazachok. He <u>brought down the house</u>.

Brenda: You're hinting that they <u>raised the roof</u>.

Martin: Yep, <u>and then some</u>. It was the most fun I've had <u>in ages</u>. And, I got to dance with Kolya's sister, the most stunning woman I've ever <u>laid eyes on</u>.

Brenda: Oh, really?

8B. Read and fill in the blanks.

From: Michael Brown <mike2@pmail.com>
Date: Thursday, March 31
To: Emily Ryan <emilyryan@sonet.com>
Subject: Politics

Em,

    How are ya? How're things in San Diego? I'm still into politics. You still working for the mayor?
    Yesterday I went to a political rally where one of the speakers caused <u>a   of</u> a row. It was a <u> mob </u>. There were <u>a</u> 5,000 people there; and when that rabble-rouser screamed, "<u> about it</u>, are you with me?" his supporters <u>raised the   </u>. After that the band <u>struck </u> the national anthem and that of course <u>brought down the   </u>. It was the most depressing show I've seen <u>in   </u>. I hope it will be years before I ever <u>   eyes on</u> that guy again, at a political event or anywhere else. He sure knows how to appeal to the worst in people.

                                                    Mike

8C. Matching Exercise. In the parentheses, write the letter of the meaning for each idiom.

Idiom

1) a good ( )
2) mob scene ( )
3) hell of a ( )
4) how about [it] ( )
5) lay eyes on ( )
6) bring down the house ( )
7) and then some ( )
8) raise the roof ( )
9) in ages ( )
10) strike up ( )

Meaning

(a) [1] Tell me about . . . [2] What's your answer?
(b) at least; fully
(c) a big crowd of people
(d) very good (or very bad)
(e) and even more
(f) for a long time
(g) to see (a person or thing)
(h) to be really noisy and rowdy
(i) to get long and loud applause for a performance
(j) to begin (playing music or conversing)

8D. Change the following sentences with an idiom from 8C.

1) That was a very bad storm. It blew down a lots of branches. _____

2) There was a big crowd at the play's opening night. _____

3) She waited for them at least two hours. _____

4) What's your answer? Do you want to come with us? _____

5) She began a conversation with a handsome student from Kenya. _____

6) Their dance routine was the biggest hit of the whole show. _____

7) They shouted and screamed when the AGs began to play their big hit. _____

8) It cost me more than a week's pay to bail her out. _____

9) Jake—you old thief! I haven't seen you in a long time. _____

10) Nope, I'd never seen him before that day. _____

The Idiom Book   17

Lesson 9
PUBLIC TRANSPORT

9A. Read.

Peter: Boy! Public transport <u>in this neck of the woods</u> <u>leaves something to be desired</u>.

Amanda: Yeah—there *is* none. You need your own car to <u>get around</u>.

Peter: I'm going to try to get someone to <u>give me a lift</u> into town; I'd like to <u>have a look at</u> some used cars I saw advertised.

Amanda: You're hopelessly <u>out of it</u>. The phrase is now "pre-owned vehicle," not "used car." <u>Get with it</u>!

Peter: Sorry. I forgot that <u>straight talk</u> has been outlawed in the world of business.

Amanda: <u>A touch</u> cynical, but you're <u>on the right track</u>.

9B. Read and fill in the blanks.

From: Peter Vogel <birdman@PSU.edu>
Date: Thursday, September 20
To: Raphael Vargas <raphaelvr@nationalU.edu>
Subject: Campus life

So how are things at NU now that you're settled in?
Life in _this_ _of the woods_ leaves _to be desired_. If you want to go to a movie or restaurant, there's no public transport. It's really hard for a student on this campus to _get_ if he has no car. A guy who rooms across the hall from me _gave_ _a lift_ into town yesterday so that I could _have a look_ a couple of used motorbikes that were advertised for sale in the college paper. I'm really _out_ it: I thought a motorbike would have a kick starter, but they all have a battery now. My roomie keeps telling me to _get_ _it_, to become more familiar with real life and the social culture in this country. He can be _touch_ acerbic, but he always gives me _straight_ and tries to keep me _on the_ _track_. I think I'll see if I can take his advice.

Pete

18 The Idiom Book

9C. Matching Exercise. In the parentheses, write the letter of the meaning for each idiom.

Idiom

1) give someone a lift ( )
2) leave something to be desired ( )
3) get around ( )
4) in this neck of the woods ( )
5) a touch ( )
6) on the right track ( )
7) out of it ( )
8) straight talk ( )
9) have a look at ( )
10) get with it ( )

Meaning

(a) to give a person a ride in a vehicle
(b) to move or travel from one place to another
(c) to be quite unsatisfactory
(d) in this area; here
(e) open, honest communication
(f) a little; somewhat
(g) thinking, or proceeding, correctly
(h) become aware of current trends or ideas
(i) unaware of one's surroundings
(j) to examine, or inspect

9D. Change the following sentences with an idiom from 9C.

1) There's not much high culture around here. _____
2) The cooking in this dorm really isn't satisfactory. _____
3) It's easy to go places if you live on campus; there's good bus service here. _____
4) A classmate of mine drove me to the airport last week. _____
5) Morning. We'd like to inspect the apartment you have for rent. _____
6) Marni was quite disoriented after the wreck. She didn't even know where she was. _____
7) You just don't know what's going on any more. You have to be more aware of current events and trends! _____
8) That politician seems incapable of saying anything in clear, simple, honest English. _____
9) I found her a little condescending. _____
10) You'll get the answer. You're going about it in the right way. _____

The Idiom Book 19

Lesson 10
AIRPORT ARRIVAL

10A. Read.

Chris: We're <u>supposed to</u> show our passport to the immigration officer.

Carol: Right. You know, a landing still <u>scares me to death</u>.

Chris: Me, too. I'm always afraid we'll <u>run out of</u> runway before we can stop.

Carol: Well, I'm always delighted that the plane's still <u>in one piece</u> when we do stop.

Chris: We've <u>made good time</u> today.

Carol: <u>Once in a blue moon</u> it happens. Should we <u>grab a bite</u> at the terminal?

Chris: No. The prices there are always <u>out of sight</u>.

Carol: If we have to wait for a gate, it could take <u>up to</u> half an hour before we start getting off.

Chris: I know. <u>Cross your fingers</u>.

10B. Read and fill in the blanks.

Journal Entry for 4/25 (in the air on Flight 3475)

We're <u>supposed</u> _____ be sophisticated travelers, you know—landing in a plane should no longer <u>scare you to</u> _____ . I know we'll still be <u>in</u> _____ piece after we hit the ground. What does bother me is the near certainty that we'll <u>run</u> _____ of money before departure day.

<u>Once</u> _____ <u>a blue moon</u> we actually <u>make</u> _____ time on one of these flights, and we've done it today! I'll be ready to _____ <u>a bite</u> as soon as we get off. I know the prices at the terminal are _____ <u>of sight</u>, but they are in town, too, and it'll probably cost us <u>up</u> _____ 50 bucks to get into the city from here. But look: We're on vacation! Forget the cost, _____ <u>your fingers</u> that we have good weather, and let's start having some fun.

20 The Idiom Book

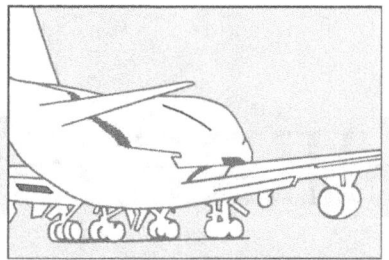

10C. Matching Exercise. In the parentheses, write the letter of the meaning for each idiom.

Idiom

1) in one piece ( )
2) scare to death ( )
3) run out of ( )
4) be supposed to ( )
5) make good time ( )
6) once in a blue moon ( )
7) up to ( )
8) cross your fingers ( )
9) grab a bite ( )
10) out of sight ( )

Meaning

(a) not hurt or damaged
(b) to use or spend all of something
(c) to terrify
(d) be expected or required to
(e) far too high; excessive
(f) as much as; as long as
(g) to make a wish for good luck
(h) to eat a small meal fast
(i) not at all often; very rarely
(j) to reach a destination on time, or early

10D. Change the following sentences with an idiom from 10C.

1) The law is that you should get the car inspected every year. _____

2) Her driving terrifies me. _____

3) I've just about spent all my money. _____

4) We walked away from the wreck OK; we're all unhurt. _____

5) He had a good trip: he got here even earlier than he thought he would. _____

6) She tries to cook a meal perhaps twice a year. _____

7) We might have just enough time to have one of those sandwiches before we board. _____

8) The food prices here are outrageous. _____

9) The cost of a sandwich here can be as high as fifteen bucks. _____

10) Make a wish that we get to the airport on time. _____

The Idiom Book

Lesson 11
GETTING THERE IS

11A. Read.

Melissa: Hi Lisa. Where were you yesterday?

Lisa: I drove to Spokane yesterday and it was <u>quite a</u> trip.

Melissa: What happened?

Lisa: The weather was, <u>suffice it to say</u>, less than optimal. <u>Off and on</u> it would snow <u>to beat hell</u> for about five minutes and then stop.

Melissa: Did you drive <u>straight through</u>?

Lisa: Well, I made a couple of <u>pit stops</u>, once to get a bite to eat and once to answer a <u>call of nature</u>. That second stop was truly <u>the pits</u>: the bathroom hadn't been cleaned in ages.

Melissa: How long did it take?

Lisa: Ten hours. When I finally walked in at my mom's, she said I looked like <u>death warmed over</u>. If she didn't live there, it's a trip <u>I'd just as soon</u> forgo.

11B. Read and fill in the blanks.

> From: Lisa Kulansky <LisaK 500@wahoo.com>
> Date: Monday, November 23
> TO: Jorge Garcia<JorgeGarcia@MSU.edu>
>
> Hi Jorge,
>
> In case you were wondering where I was yesterday, I drove to Spokane to see my mother; I had <u>quite</u> day. I wanted to drive <u>straight</u>, but it would rain and blow <u>to</u> <u>hell</u> for about ten minutes and then stop suddenly, and this happened <u>off</u> <u>on</u> all through the trip. So I had to make some <u>pit</u>.
>
> I stopped at one place to answer a <u>call</u> <u>nature</u> and the bathroom there hadn't seen a janitor in ages. That place was <u>pits</u>. Mom said that when she saw me, I looked like <u>death</u> <u>over</u>. That trip is, <u>suffice it to</u>, something <u>I'd just</u> <u>soon</u> forgo.

22 The Idiom Book

HALF THE FUN

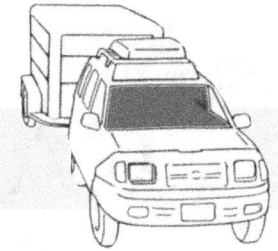

11C. Matching Exercise. In the parentheses, write the letter of the meaning for each idiom.

Idiom

1) to beat hell ( )
2) suffice it to say ( )
3) off and on ( )
4) quite a ( )
5) the pits ( )
6) call of nature ( )
7) pit stop ( )
8) death warmed over ( )
9) straight through ( )
10) 'd (would) just as soon ( )

Meaning

(a) very hard, forcefully, or extremely
(b) occasionally
(c) this is an understatement
(d) a very good, bad, unusual, or interesting person or thing
(e) without stopping
(f) someone exhausted or quite sick
(g) prefer to
(h) an extremely unpleasant place or situation
(i) a need to urinate or defecate
(j) a stop during a journey to eat or to use the toilet

11D. Change the following sentences with an idiom from 11C.

1) That was a really interesting story that she told. _____

2) It is simply enough to say it was a long drive. _____
3) He has been working on his book intermittently for about two years. _____

4) It rained very hard for an hour. _____
5) We drove from LA without stopping to San Francisco. _____

6) Let's take a break at the next service center. _____
7) Let's stop. I need to use the toilet. _____
8) That dump he lives in is a dreadful mess. _____
9) What's happened to you? You look awful! _____
10) I'd prefer to wait until we get to an exit. _____

Lesson 12
CARELESS DRIVER

12A. Read.

Peg: Pat!

Pat: What?

Peg: <u>Far be it from me</u> to criticize your driving, but you just <u>ran a red light</u>.

Pat: Any cops <u>in sight</u>?

Peg: No, I guess you're <u>home free</u>. But <u>damn it</u>—we could have <u>ended up</u> in the hospital.

Pat: Sorry. <u>I've got a lot on my plate</u> today, and I guess I shouldn't be <u>behind the wheel</u>.

Peg: Well, we're almost there. Just <u>watch it</u> at the intersections, OK?

Pat: I'll <u>keep my eyes open</u>.

12B. Read and fill in the blanks.

> From: Arthur Hall <HallFamily@homenet.com>
> To: Lola Hall <lolahall@Excel.com>
> Subject: Safety lecture
>
> Dear Lola,
>
> How goes the money blues? Are you ____ *free* yet? If not, any end ___ *sight*? I know that whopping fine that you had to pay for <u>running a</u> ___ <u>light</u> didn't help; and <u>far</u> ___ <u>it from me</u> to criticize, but you could have <u>ended</u> ___ in an ambulance or with a law suit. You're so scatterbrained that I'm not sure you should be allowed to be ____ *the wheel*, especially when you<u>'ve got a</u> ___ <u>on your plate</u> (as was the case when you committed the violation). I don't want you to leave us quite yet, so ____ *it* when you're driving. <u>Keep your</u> ____ *open*, <u>damn</u> ___!
>
> Dad

24   The Idiom Book

12C. Matching Exercise. In the parentheses, write the letter of the meaning for each idiom.

Idiom

1) far be it from me ( )
2) home free ( )
3) in sight ( )
4) run a light ( )
5) watch it ( )
6) damn it ( )
7) have (got) a lot on one's plate ( )
8) keep one's eyes open ( )
9) end up ( )
10) behind the wheel ( )

Meaning

(a) through the hardest or worst part of something
(b) [1] visible [2] likely to happen
(c) to drive past a red traffic signal and not stop
(d) I would not presume (to do something)
(e) driving a vehicle
(f) be careful
(g) to stay alert and watchful
(h) be busy with a lot of different tasks
(i) to reach a final point, result, or conclusion
(j) an expression of irritation or anger

12D. Change the following sentences with an idiom from 12C.

1) I don't want to tell you how to raise your kids, but they do have some strange table manners. _____

2) Failing to stop for a red traffic signal can be expensive. _____

3) I still don't see their car. _____

4) That was my last procedure with Dr. Schmertz. I guess I'm through the worst of it. _____

5) This is terrible!—how do we find a parking place in this madhouse? _____

6) If you're not more careful, you'll find yourself in the emergency room at Mercy Hospital. _____

7) She's busy with a lot of different things today, so try not to bother her too much. _____

8) There's a loony driving that car; she's doing about 150 KPH! _____

9) The roads are icy today, so be careful. _____

10) If you go skating on the pond tonight, look around and up: they say the stars might be visible. _____

Lesson 13
EDITOR'S OFFICE

13A. Read.

Nancy: <u>How goes it</u> with the new job?

Leslie: I'm going to work all weekend to try to <u>get rid of</u> the letter and email backlog.

Nancy: What backlog? I thought you were <u>on top of</u> things.

Leslie: I *am* current with my own stuff. These are letters the previous editor never <u>got around to</u> answering. She <u>had words</u> with the head editor over some election issue, got really <u>teed off</u> at how he described her knowledge of politics, and left without <u>giving notice.</u> I'm not really sure I can <u>fill her shoes.</u>

Nancy: Oh, you'll <u>fill the bill</u> OK.

Leslie: It's going to be tricky, <u>to say the least.</u>

13B. Read and fill in the blanks.

From: Mike Morgan <mandamorgan@speedcast.com>
Date: March 31
To: Josh Reiner <Joshr35@SSM.net>

Dear Josh,

<u>How</u> it these days? Still working for the highway department in Brookville? I thought of you today because the forecast says a norther's going to dump about a foot of snow on us tonight, but the plows should <u>get</u> of it by morning. Our road crews are pretty good at staying <u>on</u> of things in the winter; and they might even <u>get around</u> repairing my road next summer—I hope. I <u>words</u> last summer with the county road commissioner about the condition of our roads—he got <u>teed</u> at my complaint, so I dropped it. Luckily, he's <u>given</u> that he intends to retire next June, and it occurs to me that you could <u>fill</u> <u>shoes</u> quite nicely. <u>Are</u> you <u>going</u> apply for the job? I hope you do— you'd <u>fill</u> bill very well, and it would be great to see more of you, <u>to</u> the <u>least</u>.

Regards,
Mike

26 The Idiom Book

13C. Matching Exercise. In the parentheses, write the letter of the meaning for each idiom.

Idiom

1) on top of ( )
2) get rid of ( )
3) how goes it ( )
4) get around to ( )
5) to say the least ( )
6) give notice ( )
7) fill the bill ( )
8) fill someone's shoes ( )
9) teed off ( )
10) have words ( )

Meaning

(a) to find time for (doing something)
(b) in control of, or fully knowledgeable about, something
(c) to eliminate, or lose or shed, something
(d) how is it/how are you
(e) to do as well as someone you have replaced
(f) to be good enough
(g) at least
(h) [1] to tell your employer beforehand that you're going to quit [2] to give a warning
(i) angry or resentful
(j) to have an argument

13D. Change the following sentences with an idiom from 13C.

1) How are you these days? _____
2) I've got a nasty cough and I can't seem to lose it. _____
3) Both our senators are usually fully informed about immigration issues. _____
4) Grandma finally took the time to write about her childhood. _____
5) Hidei and Matt argued at the party. _____
6) For some reason, my wife was angry at my reaction to her new dress. _____
7) I've already told the boss that I'm quitting. _____
8) When the star of the musical got sick, there was no one to replace her. _____
9) If you need a beginning reader for first-graders, this book will do just fine. _____
10) This storm will at least delay all flights. _____

Lesson 14

ON THE JOB

14A. Read.

Bob: I <u>could use</u> some overtime. I think I'll go in and see if that copier is still <u>on the fritz</u>.

Chris: Well, Jason won't have fixed it. He just doesn't <u>pull his weight</u>.

Bob: That's <u>for sure</u>. <u>When it comes to</u> his personal convenience, nothing else matters; but <u>thanks to</u> his laziness, I get all the overtime I can use.

Chris: And if you <u>go out of your way</u> on a weekend to <u>make sure</u> the office equipment is <u>in good repair</u> on a Monday morning, you <u>get in good with</u> management *and* the office staff.

14B. Read and fill in the blanks.

Peg:

I'll be home at 4:30. Do me a favor and get in touch with your brother. Tell him I <u>could use</u> some help getting the firewood into the shed. The furnace is <u>on</u> the <u>fritz</u> and there's a storm coming in, so we'll need to use the fireplace tonight <u>for sure</u>. If we can get your brother to <u>pull his weight</u>, we'll finish the job in under an hour. <u>When</u> it <u>comes to</u> chores around here, you <u>go out of your way</u> to <u>make sure</u> things are <u>in good repair</u>. <u>Thanks to</u> you, the furnace is the only thing that hasn't given us trouble in a couple of years. If your brother wants to <u>get in good with</u> me again, he'll start being more like you.

Pat

28 The Idiom Book

14C. Matching Exercise. In the parentheses, write the letter of the meaning for each idiom.

Idiom

1) for sure ( )
2) on the fritz ( )
3) pull one's weight ( )
4) could use ( )
5) get in good with ( )
6) in good repair ( )
7) go out of one's way ( )
8) when it comes to ( )
9) thanks to ( )
10) make sure ( )

Meaning

(a) quite true; certain; definitely
(b) to do one's share of the work
(c) not working or operating properly
(d) to want or need something
(e) to ensure something
(f) well maintained and working properly
(g) to ingratiate oneself with someone
(h) to deliberately do more work than necessary
(i) because of
(j) when the situation entails or involves. . . .

14D. Change the following sentences with an idiom from 14C.

1) I need a good night's sleep. _____
2) The TV isn't working. _____
3) If my brother-in law does his share, we'll get the driveway shoveled fast. _____

4) We're definitely leaving for Tokyo next Sunday. _____

5) When it's time to do the dishes, Art's usually very busy with schoolwork. _____

6) Because of this wretched weather, we'll have to cancel our picnic. _____

7) Ayla works extra hard for us whenever we need help. _____

8) She always ensures that every document has been edited and filed properly. _____

9) They've got a first-class mechanic; he keeps all the machinery working right. _____

10) My brother's trying to get his pretty new classmate to notice him and like him. _____

Lesson 15

FAMILY

15A. Read.

Liz: It looks like cousin Bob is here, and Cousin Lola <u>as well.</u>

Carol: Was it last year that she brought that guy about 13 years <u>her junior?</u>

Liz: Yes. She does like to <u>make an entrance</u> at these affairs.

Carol: I <u>couldn't help</u> noticing that Great-Aunt Mabel looks as if she's <u>at death's door.</u>

Liz: That's just her awful complexion—she's never looked healthy but she really is. And she's as sharp as ever: she tells me her latest book is <u>shaping up</u> pretty well.

Carol: That woman is <u>something else.</u>

Liz: Yep. She's <u>one of a kind.</u> Eighty-six years old and still not ready to <u>pack it in.</u>

Carol: <u>Would that</u> we had more relatives like her.

15B. Read and fill in the blanks.

Journal entry for May 28

Aunt Tilly is a character. She speaks Russian, German, English, and now a little Japanese <u>well</u>. She enjoyed her Japanese lessons immensely: her Japanese tutor was ten years _____ <u>junior</u>, and when those two came into the center together in the morning, they would <u>make</u> quite _____ <u>entrance</u>. You <u>couldn't</u> _____ noticing the special attention he paid to her. Now he's back in Osaka, and she looks as if she's <u>at death's</u> _____. Heartache, I guess.

My ESL class is _____ up very nicely. I have a student from Shanghai who's _____ <u>else</u>. She's brilliant, beautiful, very funny, and an accomplished pianist. Indeed, the class is almost <u>one</u> _____ <u>a kind</u>; the students are all so interesting that I should pay to be with them rather than they to be with me. The school administration is so inept and unhelpful that I was almost ready to <u>pack</u> _____ in last week, but the students make it all worthwhile. _____ that every teacher could say that.

30   The Idiom Book

15C. Matching Exercise. In the parentheses, write the letter of the meaning for each idiom.

Idiom

1) one's junior ( )
2) as well ( )
3) can't help -ing ( )
4) make an entrance ( )
5) at death's door ( )
6) would that ( )
7) one of a kind ( )
8) something else ( )
9) shaping up ( )
10) pack it in ( )

Meaning

(a) to be unable to avoid being or doing something
(b) to arrive dramatically
(c) younger (than her or him)
(d) also
(e) unique
(f) to quit doing something, especially work
(g) I wish [that]. . . . ; if only
(h) almost extraordinary
(i) developing; proceeding; progressing
(j) almost dead

15D. Change the following sentences with an idiom from 15C.

1) And she's also better trained than I am. _____

2) My new boss is ten years younger than I am. _____

3) When Uncle Max comes into a room, it's like the arrival of an Eastern king. _____

4) It was impossible to miss the looks that Yuko and Mike were exchanging at the party. _____

5) It's awful. He looks as if he has terminal cancer. _____

6) My book's proceeding pretty well. I've already finished 80 lessons. _____

7) That politician is a rare bird: She's honest, intelligent, and well-educated. _____

8) There's nobody else like him. He actually keeps his promises. _____

9) This job of mine isn't much fun any more. I'm about ready to quit. _____

10) I used to be able to hike ten miles. I wish I could relive those days. _____

Lesson 16

EXERCISE

16A. Read.

Pablo: Tomo, I <u>wouldn't mind</u> some exercise. Let's go bowling.
Tomo: Bowling is really <u>not my thing</u>, you know.
Pablo: That's OK. I'll <u>show you the ropes</u>.

****

Tomo: Here we are. You first, Pablo.
Pablo: No, you <u>go ahead</u>, Tomo.
Tomo: God! That ball <u>missed by a mile</u>.
Pablo: Well, it was <u>nothing to write home about</u>, but <u>all in all</u> you're going to do OK. You'll <u>get the hang of it</u>.
Tomo: That <u>remains to be seen</u>.
Pablo: Hey, <u>cut yourself some slack</u>. You're just beginning.

16B. Read and fill in the blanks.

> From: Robert Jones rjones@socal.net
> To: Amanda Jones ajjones@socal.net
> Subject: The Lake House
> My Dear Amanda,
>
> Jake and I are having a great time here at the lake. Sorry you couldn't come this weekend. The weather is great.
>
> You know, I <u>wouldn't</u> _____ buying this place, if we could afford it. (Maybe they'd apply some of the past rent to the purchase price?) Schmoozing with the owners is <u>not</u> really <u>my</u> _____, but I suppose you could <u>show me</u> _____ <u>ropes</u>.
>
> Jake and I decided to <u>go</u> _____ and saw the firewood. He had his shotgun with him, and took a shot at a wild turkey that landed about a hundred feet away. He <u>missed</u> _____ <u>a mile</u>, and I took the opportunity to suggest to him that his marksmanship was <u>nothing</u> _____ <u>write home about</u>. He didn't like that.
>
> You know, <u>all</u> _____ <u>all</u> I really do like it here, and I'm starting to <u>get the</u> _____ <u>of</u> maintaining the place. Of course <u>it</u> _____ <u>to be seen</u> whether we could swing it, but <u>cut me some</u> _____ and at least let me fantasize for a while about owning it.
>
> I miss you. Wish you were here.
>
> R.

16C. Matching Exercise. In the parentheses, write the letter of the meaning for each idiom.

Idiom

1) not one's thing ( )
2) wouldn't mind ( )
3) show someone the ropes ( )
4) go ahead ( )
5) all in all ( )
6) nothing to write home about ( )
7) by a mile ( )
8) cut someone some slack ( )
9) remains to be seen ( )
10) get the hang of something ( )

Meaning

(a) to proceed or continue
(b) to teach someone a task or activity
(c) not very good, skilled, or interested in something
(d) would like being or doing something
(e) to learn, gradually, how to do something
(f) is still uncertain, unclear, or unknown
(g) to not criticize someone; give someone leeway
(h) generally
(i) not really very good
(j) a lot; greatly

16D. Change the following sentences with an idiom from 16C.

1) I'd like a piece of that pie. _____
2) No thanks. I'm not very good at karaoke. _____
3) There's no problem using the mike—I'll teach you how to do it. _____
4) You go first; I'll follow you. —————
5) He took a shot but didn't even hit the basket. _____
6) That performance of his at the concert was mediocre. _____
7) Generally, it hasn't been too bad a year. _____
8) If you ski at least once a week, you'll finally become pretty good at it. _____
9) Whether your evaluation is accurate is as yet unknown. _____
10) I know he didn't do well, but it's not fair to criticize him like that: he's only played a few times. _____

The Idiom Book

Lesson 17
A CHILLY ROMANCE

17A. Read.

Bob: Hi, Evan. I've got something to tell you.
Evan: So, what's up, Bob?
Bob: Annie and I <u>took a spin</u> over to Breakneck Acres Sunday.
Evan: Is that a motorcycle track or a bar?
Bob: It's a ski area, <u>wise guy</u>.
Evan: You two have <u>been known to</u> frequent both kinds of places, you know.
Bob: <u>Get off my back</u>!
Evan: No need to <u>take offense</u>. Please continue.
Bob: Well, we both <u>crashed and burned</u> as often as we made it to the bottom on our feet, but we had a grand time.
Evan: You two always have a grand time, and somehow I think I <u>have yet</u> to hear the <u>punch line</u> of this story.
Bob: We're going skiing again tomorrow, and I'm going to <u>pop the question</u>.
Evan: Wow! Now you're <u>in for it</u>!

17B. Read and fill in the blanks.

> From: Robert Gonzales robgon@supernet.com
> To: Ken Suzuki <KenjiSuz@moonlink.com>
> Subject: Yuko
>
> So here's what's new with us. We _____ <u>a spin</u> up into the hills in Yuko's convertible yesterday and had a great time. A <u>wise</u> _____ at a gas station gave us wrong directions for getting to the restaurant, but we found it anyway. He also made a rude comment on Yuko's car and my ponytail but I told him to <u>get off</u> _____ <u>back</u> (I do <u>take</u> _____ at deliberate rudeness.).
> That place is so beautiful that people have <u>been</u> _____ <u>to</u> fall in love under its spell, and I think I succumbed. So I was feeling pretty good even though I <u>crashed and</u> _____ on my calculus exam last week, but yesterday with Yuko sure helped to ease the pain. I <u>have</u> _____ to actually flunk a whole course, and I think I can handle this one: I've learned to laugh uproariously at the <u>punch</u> _____ of the instructor's jokes.
> I suppose some "friends" might tell Yuko that she's <u>in</u> _____ <u>it</u> when they learn that I've <u>popped</u> _____ <u>question</u>. I hope she doesn't agree.
>
> Bob

34   The Idiom Book

17C. Matching Exercise. In the parentheses write the letter of the meaning for each idiom.

Idiom

1) wise guy ( )
2) take a spin ( )
3) be known to ( )
4) get off one's back ( )
5) take offense ( )
6) pop the question ( )
7) in for it ( )
8) punch line ( )
9) crash and burn ( )
10) have yet ( )

Meaning

(a) Stop! Enough!
(b) to have a habit that people know about
(c) an annoying person who likes to say sarcastic or cynical things
(d) to go for a short ride in, or on, a wheeled vehicle
(e) the last part of a joke or story, which makes it funny or surprising
(f) to ask someone to marry you
(g) sure to be punished
(h) have not yet done something
(i) to fail, or fall, badly
(j) to get mad, or be offended

17D. Change each of the following sentences with an idiom from 17C.

1) I rode my new bike around the reservoir yesterday. _____

2) That clown's a real jerk: his favorite pastime is making sarcastic comments. _____

3) There's no denying it, Sotby. We all know you like to have an occasional drink. _____

4) Stop! I don't want to hear any more about that. _____

5) They shouldn't get mad at our youthful, high-spirited joking. _____

6) I went snowboarding yesterday and I fell, disastrously and spectacularly, on my first three attempts. _____

7) I've owned a PC for seven years and still haven't learned how to change the margins. _____

8) You know, if she told the funny part of that joke, I either didn't hear it or didn't understand it. _____

9) Ali and Karen spent all day Sunday together. I think he's going to ask her to marry him. ___

10) Hmm. If she accepts, he's going to suffer. _____

Lesson 18
LOCAL CUISINE

18A. Read.

Dave: Hello.

Phil: Hey Dave. How are ya. It's Phil.

Dave: Hi Phil, What's up?

Phil: Well, where do you and Alice go when you want to <u>eat out</u>?

Dave: We used to eat out <u>from time to time</u>, but we don't now. It's too expensive and the choices <u>around here</u> are not that great.

Phil: The same with us. <u>One of these days</u> I'm going to <u>open up</u> my own restaurant and offer good food at low prices.

Dave: That sounds like a good way to <u>lose your shirt</u>. The competition would <u>eat you alive</u>.

Phil: But there isn't any competition <u>to speak of</u>. Most places in town are either chains or <u>greasy spoons</u>—their food just doesn't <u>make the grade</u>.

18B. Read and fill in the blanks.

This is 256-7771. Please leave a message.

Hi Anne, I'll be home soon. As for dinner, let's <u>eat</u>   this evening. So far, we haven't had much snow <u>to</u>   <u>of</u>, but we're going to get a lot late tonight and <u>from time to</u>   the roads <u>around</u>   are blocked for a few days; we don't go out much these days, so let's try that new Thai restaurant that just _____ <u>up</u>. There won't be a lot of people there because of the weather, so we won't have to wait for a table and we can hope it's not just another <u>greasy</u>   . Mike ate there the night he <u>lost his</u>   at the casino; he said his blackjack dealer <u>ate</u>   <u>alive</u>, but at least the Thai food did <u>make</u>   <u>grade</u>. <u>One</u>   <u>these days</u>, he might admit to himself he's got a gambling problem. See you soon.

18C. Matching Exercise. In the parentheses write the letter of the meaning for each idiom.

Idiom

1) around here (   )
2) one of these days (   )
3) eat out (   )
4) from time to time (   )
5) greasy spoon (   )
6) to speak of (   )
7) make the grade (   )
8) open up (   )
9) lose one's shirt (   )
10) eat someone alive (   )

Meaning

(a) at some time in the future
(b) occasionally
(c) in this place/town/area
(d) to eat in a restaurant
(e) worth mentioning; of importance
(f) a cheap restaurant that sells a lot of fried food
(g) to be good enough
(h) to defeat or ruin an opponent decisively
(i) to lose all of one's money in business or gambling
(j) to begin operating (a new business)

18D. Change each of the following sentences with an idiom from 18C.

1) I can't afford to eat in restaurants. _____
2) Did you stop occasionally on your trip? _____
3) Some really screwy things are happening in this place. _____
4) Someday I'm going to tell the boss what I think of her. _____
5) A new Bloatmart store just started doing business at the mall. _____
6) My brother lost all his money in one of the dot-com scams. _____
7) She's a hard worker, but her competitors drove her out of business in a year. _____
8) This town doesn't have much crime worth mentioning. _____
9) We stopped at a place that sells a lot of hamburgers and fries. _____
10) Smedley, your work just isn't good enough. _____

Lesson 19
JOB INTERVIEW

19A. Read.

Harry: Morning. I'm Harry Hopewell. I think Mr. Bosse is expecting me to <u>put in an appearance</u> this morning.

Receptionist: Oh yes, Mr. Hopewell. Mr. Bosse has <u>put</u> everything else <u>on hold</u> to make time for your interview. He should be with you in ten minutes, <u>more or less</u>.

****

Bosse: Good morning, Mr. Hopewell. I'm Boswell Bosse—I run the advertising section here.

Harry: Good morning, sir. Thanks for seeing me <u>on such short notice</u>.

Bosse: <u>My pleasure</u>. Your resume looked interesting to me.

Harry: Um, did you <u>have in mind</u> something specific for me, sir?

Bosse: Well, possibly. One of our writers is <u>getting on in years</u> and wants to retire. I need someone like you who might <u>take up the slack</u> when she leaves.

Harry: I'm flattered that you think I might be good enough to <u>take her place</u>.

Bosse: Don't assume it's <u>in the bag</u> yet, but I'd like you to come in Tuesday to meet the other writers.

19B. Read and fill in the blanks.

January 15

Dear Pop,

I ____ <u>in an appearance</u> at the inauguration ceremony yesterday. They <u>put everything</u> ____ <u>hold</u> for <u>more</u> ____ <u>less</u> 20 minutes because the PA system wouldn't work, but they finally got it going. I was summoned there <u>on</u> ____ <u>notice</u> because my boss got sick and they wanted somebody there from our department. They of course thanked me profusely, and I of course responded, "____ <u>pleasure</u>," but honoring that buffoon with my presence was not something I'd <u>had</u> ____ <u>mind</u> for yesterday morning. The chief justice is <u>getting</u> ____ <u>in years</u>, but he gave a mercifully short speech; I think it'll be pretty easy to find someone to <u>take</u> ____ <u>the slack</u> when he retires. What I'd really like to see happen is for someone to ____ <u>the president's place</u>, but then of course his replacement would be the VP, who's even worse. You know, Pop, with the way the country seems to have changed, I'm not sure that even after eight years of these guys the next election will be <u>in</u> ____ <u>bag</u> for us.

Love,
H.

38 The Idiom Book

19C. Matching Exercise. In the parentheses write the letter of the meaning for each idiom.

Idiom

1) put something on hold ( )
2) more or less ( )
3) on short notice ( )
4) put in an appearance ( )
5) take up the slack ( )
6) in the bag ( )
7) get on in years ( )
8) my pleasure ( )
9) take someone's place ( )
10) have in mind ( )

Meaning

(a) without warning or advance notice
(b) about, approximately
(c) to delay, or postpone something
(d) to attend; be present
(e) to do work that someone else has been doing
(f) to replace someone
(g) achieved, assured, or won
(h) to become old
(i) to contemplate, consider, or think about
(j) you're quite welcome

19D. Change each of the following sentences with an idiom from 19C.

1) I went to the funeral. _____
2) We'll have to delay our expansion plans for a while. _____
3) We have about thirty people working on this project. _____
4) She kindly and graciously agreed to interview me without much advance warning. _____
5) "Thanks a lot for your help." "You're quite welcome." _____
6) Just what is it that you're thinking about doing? _____
7) Uncle Fudd is getting old: he forgot to put on his pants this morning. _____
8) Laura's our best worker. If she leaves, who's going to do her work? _____
9) We'll find someone to replace her. It'll just take a little time. _____
10) We're three goals ahead—the game's won! _____

Lesson 20
CUTTING CORNERS

20A. Read.

Skinner: You know, Buncome, <u>between you and me</u>, we'll have to cheat on our taxes this year <u>so as</u> to <u>break even</u>.
Buncome: And I think we'll have to stop some of the employee benefits <u>to boot</u>.
Skinner: Only <u>as a last resort</u>.
Buncome: Of course. We'll find a way to <u>cut corners</u> that won't do too much damage.
Skinner: Right. We're <u>on the same page</u>, then. I think we should start by trading in the company SUVs for compact hybrids.
Buncome: Ooh! You *do* <u>mean business</u>.
Skinner: Well, if we tell our people that everyone has to sacrifice, we should <u>put our money where our mouth is</u>.
Buncome: Skinner, you might <u>have the makings of</u> a decent manager someday.

20B. Read and fill in the blanks.

From: Herbert Walker <GHW3@baylink.com>
To: George Walker <GWalkerson@Aceserv.com>
Subject: Congratulations

Georgie,

Congratulations on your appointment with INS. When I worked as an immigration officer at the airport, I would always talk to any little kids with incoming passengers <u>so</u> to make sure they hadn't been kidnapped. When I just couldn't understand, I could always call an interpreter <u>as a</u> <u>resort</u>. Quite often, four- and five-year-olds would jabber away, and quite charm me and then offer me candy <u>boot</u>.

You know, the immigration service is supposed to be self-supporting, and sometimes we would inspect five jumbo jets in a row without a break as a way to <u>corners</u> and <u>break</u> for that day. The immigration managers <u>mean</u> when the bottom line—the number of passengers inspected—is involved; and <u>between</u> <u>and me</u> the quality of the passenger inspections is not quite as important for them. The managers and the officers are rarely <u>on the same</u> : the managers have to deal with statistics and the officers with people. A person like you who's interested in people and who speaks a couple of foreign languages may <u>have</u> <u>makings of</u> a good immigration officer.

I've been saying to friends for a long time that our immigration officers are too few to handle the flood of people that come into this country all the time. I think I'll <u>put my money where my</u> <u>is</u> and write about it to my senators and to the *Times*.

Uncle Herbert

20C. Matching Exercise. In the parentheses write the letter of the meaning for each idiom.

Idiom

1) between you and me ( )
2) to boot ( )
3) break even ( )
4) so as ( )
5) cut corners ( )
6) as a last resort ( )
7) on the same page ( )
8) mean business ( )
9) have the makings of ( )
10) put your money where your mouth is ( )

Meaning

(a) also
(b) to not lose money
(c) for this reason:
(d) confidentially, secretly
(e) to be serious
(f) support with action what one believes in
(g) be able to become something
(h) thinking about, or working on, the same thing
(i) to economize
(j) if everything else fails; if nothing else works or succeeds

20D. Change each of the following sentences with an idiom from 20C.

1) Don't tell anyone, but I think we're facing a big loss this year. _____

2) We always call first for this reason: to make sure they're expecting us. _____

3) She managed not to lose money in her first year in business. _____

4) She made a little money, and also a lot of new customers. _____

5) I guess I can ask my brother for a loan if nothing else works. _____

6) If we economize, we can avoid firing anybody. _____

7) Just to be sure we all have the same idea, we have to save money without losing workers! _____

8) Boy, she's serious about cutting costs. _____

9) If you really mean that, we have to set an example. _____

10) He might become a pretty good salesman. _____

The Idiom Book 41

Lesson 21

HIKING

21A. Read.

Betsy: This weather's <u>made to order</u> for a hike up Mount Pleasant.

Fred: I don't know if I'm <u>in the mood</u> for it.

Betsy: Sure you are! And anyway, you <u>could do with</u> some exercise. That <u>spare tire</u> isn't shrinking.

Fred: Hey! I have feelings, you know. So, OK, I'll go, but I want you to know that you're <u>twisting my arm</u>.

Betsy: Well, it won't hurt you to do this. I'll make some sandwiches, if you'll <u>see to</u> the drinks.

[Up on the mountain.]

Fred: Well, we <u>made short work of</u> those sandwiches. They <u>hit the spot</u>.

Betsy: They were <u>just what the doctor ordered</u>.

Fred: I think <u>I'd rather</u> be up here in this beautiful spot, with you, than any place else in the world.

Betsy: Really?

21B. Read and fill in the blanks.

Journal Entry June 15

The situation was <u>made</u> _____ order for a quick trip to Chicago. We had a three-day weekend, and I was <u>in</u> _____ <u>mood</u> for something different, and <u>could do</u> _____ a change. (And I thought running to catch buses and trains might help me reduce this <u>spare</u> _____.). I <u>made</u> _____ work of the chores I had left to do and called her. I knew that she would go only of I <u>twisted her</u> _____ , so I made a reservation at a four-star hotel and I _____ <u>to</u> the train tickets and met her at the station at seven in the morning.

It was a grand weekend: it was <u>just what the</u> _____ <u>ordered</u>. The restaurants <u>hit</u> _____ <u>spot</u>; although the cost staggered me a bit. Given a choice, <u>I'd</u> _____ be with her than anyone else in the world.

42   The Idiom Book

21C. Matching Exercise. In the parentheses write the letter of the meaning for each idiom.

Idiom

1) made to order ( )
2) spare tire ( )
3) could do with ( )
4) in the mood ( )
5) make short work of ( )
6) see to ( )
7) twist someone's arm ( )
8) hit the spot ( )
9) 'd rather [would rather] ( )
10) just what the doctor ordered ( )

Meaning

(a) a man's fat belly
(b) to need something
(c) ready to be or do something
(d) ideal, or perfect
(e) to taste very good
(f) exactly what you needed or wanted
(g) prefer to
(h) to finish or use something quickly
(i) to attend to something
(j) force someone to do something

21D. Change each of the following sentences with an idiom from 21C.

1) Boy, this job is *ideal* for me. _____
2) I don't feel like socializing tonight. _____
3) This room needs a coat of paint. _____
4) Tom looks a bit overweight with that beer belly of his. _____

5) I'm only going to that faculty tea because you're forcing me to. _____

6) If you set up the tables and chairs, I'll fix the sandwiches. _____

7) The kids sure ate that ice cream fast. _____
8) Man, that beer tasted good. _____
9) After working hard on a cold day, a cup of tea is just what I need. _____

10) I've been invited to go to her recital, but I prefer to clean the garage. _____

Lesson 22

USED CAR

22A. Read.

Joe: My old car's <u>on its last legs</u> and I've got to replace it. And getting a used car is like getting <u>a pig in a poke</u>. You never know what to expect.

Roger: And you think a used car dealer will always try to <u>pull a fast one on</u> you, but I know a gal down at Wreck-Mart who's strictly <u>on the up and up</u>.

Joe: Sorry, I don't believe it. Lying <u>comes with the territory</u>.

Roger: No, really. She'll give you <u>the real scoop</u> on her cars. <u>Take my word for it</u>: she's actually honest.

[At the used car dealer.]

Joe: You understand that I have to find something <u>within my means</u>.

Penny: We're asking an even grand for this baby. Is that <u>in the ballpark</u>?

Joe: Why, that car's <u>at least</u> as old as I am!

22B. Read and fill in the blanks.

MEMO

TO: Rick Bartleby   DATE: August 23
FROM: Bill Brown   RE: Your copier

Bartleby, I know your copier's <u>on its   legs</u>, and you need a new one. Now, there's an office-equipment auction downtown this week, but if you buy something from one of those you're always getting <u>a   in a poke</u>, especially if the auctioneer is one of those people who's always ready to <u>   a fast one</u>, a slippery character who's just not <u>on the   and up</u>, who's unwilling to give you <u>the   scoop</u> on something (s)he's trying to sell. You're the writer here, and ensuring that the printer works <u>comes   the territory</u>; but <u>take my   for it</u>, that auction's a good place to stay away from. Whatever and wherever you buy, be sure you get something that's <u>within our   </u>. Something like $1,500 would be <u>   the ballpark</u>. There are <u>   least</u> half a dozen places in town that sell computers and printers, so go for it.

---

44 The Idiom Book

22C. Matching Exercise. In the parentheses write the letter of the meaning for each idiom.

Idiom

1) pull a fast one ( )
2) a pig in a poke ( )
3) on its last legs ( )
4) on the up and up ( )
5) within one's means ( )
6) the real scoop ( )
7) take my word for it ( )
8) at least ( )
9) in the ballpark ( )
10) comes with the territory ( )

Meaning

(a) honest
(b) to deceive or trick someone
(c) something of unknown value
(d) almost useless because of age or wear
(e) cheap enough; affordable
(f) approximately correct; close enough
(g) no less than; no fewer than
(h) believe me
(i) the truth
(j) to be an integral, or unavoidable, part of something

22D. Change each of the following sentences with an idiom from 22C.

1) This conveyor is so old and worn it's almost useless. _____

2) You're taking a chance when you buy an "antique" from her. _____

3) The dealer I bought my used car from tricked me—he turned back the odometer. _____

4) You can trust her. She's honest. _____

5) Learning to cope with unreliable suppliers is part of my job. _____

6) I've got the real facts on what happened at Dodsworth & Company. _____

7) Believe me, sir—you'll love this car. _____

8) No, I don't want that computer. It's too expensive for me. _____

9) My guess is that the arena holds around a thousand people. Is that about right? _____

10) That house is no less than 100 years old. _____

Lesson 23

SPRING

23A. Read.

Chuck: Winter <u>in these parts</u> really <u>does a number on</u> the property. There's stuff <u>all over</u> my backyard. I hate this.

Art: Yeah, it <u>messed up</u> my place too, but I'm still glad to see spring here. The chipmunks are back <u>in force</u> and the old tomcat is again chasing them, again <u>to no avail</u>. The world is starting to <u>come to life</u> again, and the threat of busted pipes is <u>at last</u> receding. I love it!

Chuck: You know, old friend, sometimes I wonder if tree huggers like you are <u>all there</u>.

Art: And <u>now and again</u>, old chum, I sorrow to admit to myself that you have the soul of a potato.

23B. Read and fill in the blanks.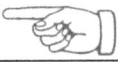

> To: Ruby Goldsmith <RVGoldsmith@Hyperlog.com>
> From: Donald Trumper <DTrumper 55@supersend.com>
> Subject: My heart
>
> Ruby,
>
> When you left the dance with that dude from Kansas City, you <u>did a number</u> my heart, as I'm sure you meant to. But it happens that there are good-looking available women out <u>in</u> at dances <u>in</u> <u>parts</u>—they're <u>over</u> the place—and I'm sure that dude will eventually notice one of them and <u>mess you</u>, too. You'll wait for his phone call <u>to</u> <u>avail</u>, as I did for yours. When <u>last</u> you realize what you did, you'll wonder if you were <u>there</u> when you decided to leave me. In a little while my shock and numbness will disappear, and my capacity for emotional attachment, for feeling affection will <u>come</u> life again. And perhaps you'll think of me <u>and again</u>.
>
> Regretfully,
>
> Donald

23C. Matching Exercise. In the parentheses write the letter of the meaning for each idiom.

Idiom

1) do a number on ( )
2) in these parts ( )
3) mess up ( )
4) all over ( )
5) all there ( )
6) come to life ( )
7) to no avail ( )
8) in force ( )
9) at last ( )
10) now and again ( )

Meaning

(a) to create disorder, discomfort, or a problem
(b) everywhere in or on something
(c) to hurt or damage someone or something
(d) in this area; around here
(e) completely sane
(f) to become alive and active
(g) occasionally
(h) finally
(i) uselessly; ineffectively/useless; ineffective
(j) in big numbers; in a big group

23D. Change each of the following sentences with an idiom from 23C.

1) In winter, ice hockey is popular around here. _____

2) The salt spread on the roads here in winter damages car bodies. _____

3) It covers the cars as well as the roads. _____

4) That last storm really caused a lot of problems with my travel plans. _____

5) At the first snow here, snowmobilers appear in huge numbers. _____

6) Farmers erect "No Trespassing" signs that are ineffective and useless. _____

7) It's glorious when the world again becomes a living thing in the spring. _____

8) When spring finally arrives, the woods are a lot quieter. _____

9) Some snowmobilers go out on a lake covered with thin ice; I'm not sure they're sane. _____

10) I occasionally go for a snowmobile ride myself. _____

The Idiom Book   47

Lesson 24
NEW APARTMENT

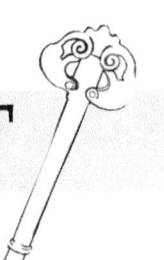

24A. Read.

Betty: Downtown Realty, Betty speaking.

Alison: Hi Betty, it's Alison and I'm looking for a new place.

Betty: Really? Why's that?

Alison: The super here <u>won't lift a finger</u> unless we bribe him, so we're going to move.

Betty: <u>How come</u> that lazy guy doesn't <u>get the axe</u>?

Alison: His brother-in-law owns the building, so <u>he's got a lock on</u> the job.

Betty: OK. I <u>get the picture</u>.

Alison: We need a two-bedroomer because Jon's mom visits <u>every now and then</u>, and we'd like it to be within five kilometers <u>or so</u> of the college, so <u>keep an eye out for</u> that kind of place, would you?

Betty: <u>Will do</u>. I'll call you <u>right away</u> if I find something likely.

24B. Read and fill in the blanks.

A Note from Winnie Luciano

September 25

Dear Mom,

Mike is so lazy around the house! He <u>won't</u> _____ <u>a finger</u> to help with any of the chores—won't even wash the dishes. <u>How</u> _____ men are so selfish? If being a spouse were a regular paid position, he'd have <u>got</u> _____ <u>axe</u> within a week, but of course he doesn't have to worry because <u>he's got a</u> _____ <u>on</u> the job. He thinks. I'd been a bit uncertain of his take on marriage, but now I'm beginning to _____ <u>the picture</u>: I work full time outside the home (and earn more money than he does) *and* I'm his live-in maid, cook, and housekeeper. <u>Every now</u> _____ <u>then</u>—once a month _____ <u>so</u>—I do get taken to a movie. So please _____ <u>an eye out</u> for a nice little apartment that you think I might like and call me _____ <u>away</u> if you find one. If you still want me to go to Taipei with you this spring, _____ <u>do</u>.

Love,
Winnie

48 The Idiom Book

24C. Matching Exercise. In the parentheses write the letter of the meaning for each idiom.

Idiom

1) won't lift a finger ( )
2) how come ( )
3) have/get a lock on something ( )
4) get the axe ( )
5) will do ( )
6) keep an eye out for ( )
7) or so ( )
8) every now and then ( )
9) get the picture ( )
10) right away ( )

Meaning

(a) to have an exclusive right to something
(b) to be fired, or discharged, from a job; lose a job
(c) why is it that. . . . ?
(d) refuses to do any work to help someone
(e) to watch carefully for something
(f) yes, of course I will
(g) immediately
(h) approximately
(i) occasionally
(j) to understand

24D. Change each of the following sentences with an idiom from 24C.

1) That lazy slob will never help me. _____
2) Why is it that you never get your homework done on time? _____
3) Globalization: I got fired! _____
4) A federal employee used to have a guaranteed lifetime job. _____
5) Oh—I understand: You just don't want to see me any more. _____
6) We see them socially occasionally. _____
7) It's about 100 kilometers from here to Chiba. _____
8) Try to spot a nice place for a picnic. _____
9) "Please get these crates loaded by noon." "Yes, of course I will." _____
10) If she develops a fever, call me immediately. _____

Lesson 25
VISIT TO THE DOCTOR

25A. Read.

[Telephone rings]

Andy: Morning. My name's Andy Unfall. I <u>took a spill</u> on my bike yesterday and this morning I'm all <u>black and blue</u>. I'd like the doctor to <u>look me over</u> and see if she can give me a <u>clean bill of health</u>, <u>as it were</u>.

Receptionist: Could you <u>make it</u> in here tomorrow at nine, Mr. Unfall?

Andy: Sure. <u>Much obliged</u>. See you in the morning.

[Next day]

Doctor: Morning Mr. Unfall. I understand you're not feeling <u>up to par</u>.

Andy: Yeah. I fell off my bike a couple of days ago and my right elbow and hip hurt <u>like hell</u>.

Doctor: Uh-huh. It sounds as if some X-rays are <u>in order</u> before we do anything else.

25B. Read and fill in the blanks.

> To: Patrick O'Brien <obrienlaw@statenet.com>
> From: J. Richard Lufkin <jrlufkin@wondernet.org>
> Subject: me and the meeting
>
> Hi Pat,
>
> I almost called you yesterday. I _____ <u>a</u> bad <u>spill</u> on the ice in front of a grocery store a couple of days ago and I wanted to sue them for negligence, but unfortunately—<u>as</u> _____ were—the doc looked me _____ and has given me a <u>clean</u> _____ <u>of health</u>, so I have no cause of action. I'm still not <u>up</u> _____ <u>par</u>, though: my shoulder is all <u>black</u> _____ <u>blue</u> and hurts _____ <u>hell</u>.
>
> Anyway, I hope you can <u>make</u> ____ to the meeting Thursday night. It seems to me a vote is <u>in</u> _____ on whether to keep Fleecewell as our treasurer.
>
> And <u>much</u> _____ for the fruitcake. It wouldn't be Christmas without it.
>
> J R

50   The Idiom Book

25C. Matching Exercise. In the parentheses write the letter of the meaning for each idiom.

Idiom

1) clean bill of health ( )
2) black and blue ( )
3) look someone/thing over ( )
4) take a spill ( )
5) up to par ( )
6) like hell ( )
7) much obliged ( )
8) as it were ( )
9) make it ( )
10) in order ( )

Meaning

(a) an official report that someone is healthy
(b) inspect or examine
(c) badly bruised
(d) to fall off skis or a bike
(e) healthy; satisfactory; good
(f) appropriate; suitable; necessary
(g) a lot, intensely
(h) thanks
(i) to reach a destination; arrive
(j) [This is often an apology for a pun or expression that the speaker just used.]

25D. Change each of the following sentences with an idiom from 25C.

1) She fell when she was roller skating. _____
2) Her knee was badly bruised from the fall. _____
3) About your report: I read it and think it's pretty good. _____
4) The doctor's written assessment is that I'm in good health. _____
5) That incense stinks to high heaven, and pardon my play on words. _____
6) Did they get back on time? _____
7) You've helped a lot. Thanks. _____
8) I don't feel good. I'm not going to go on the hike. _____
9) Ooh! That tack really hurt. _____
10) I think a pause for refreshments would be appropriate right about now. _____

The Idiom Book 51

Lesson 26

BAD DOG

26A. Read.

Brent: I ride my bike to work, and almost <u>every other day</u> the dog from the corner house chases me <u>with an eye to</u> <u>tearing me limb from limb</u>. Unless I <u>take steps</u> to discourage the brute, <u>it's only a matter of time</u> before it succeeds.

Bev: Call the owner and tell her the dog's <u>out of control</u>.

Brent: Oh, she's <u>off her rocker</u>. She and the dog <u>make a good pair</u>.

Bev: Then you<u>'d better</u> call the animal control officer.

Brent: <u>I suppose so</u>.

26B. Read and fill in the blanks.

JOURNAL FOR May 13

<u>Every</u> _____ <u>day</u> I check the newspaper notices of bankruptcy sales of real estate <u>with an</u> _____ <u>to</u> buying something, repairing it, and making a nice profit. My wife would <u>tear me limb</u> _____ <u>limb</u> if she knew I was thinking about it, and <u>it's only a</u> _____ <u>of time</u> before she discovers my interest. When she does, she'll say I'm <u>off</u> _____ <u>rocker</u>, and I'm really _____ <u>of control</u>, and will probably _____ <u>steps</u> to separate all her property from mine, chiefly by filing for divorce.

When I recently asked her if she'd like to take a cruise on the Caribbean, she responded, "<u>I suppose</u> _____." Her wild enthusiasm made me think <u>I</u> _____ <u>better</u> be seriously prepared for a split, whatever I do or don't do. As models of how not to be good spouses, she and I <u>make a</u> _____ <u>pair</u>.

26C. Matching Exercise. In the parentheses write the letter of the meaning for each idiom.

Idiom

1) every other day ( )
2) tear someone limb from limb ( )
3) with an eye to ( )
4) take steps ( )
5) I suppose so ( )
6) make a good pair ( )
7) off one's rocker ( )
8) out of control ( )
9) 'd (had) better ( )
10) it's only a matter of time ( )

Meaning

(a) act decisively and deliberately
(b) [1] to tear someone's body apart [2] attack someone verbally
(c) with the hope or intention of (doing something)
(d) once every two days
(e) are like each other in some way
(f) should
(g) yes [often unenthusiastic]
(h) crazy
(i) impossible to control; wild
(j) there's only limited time

26D. Change each of the following sentences with an idiom from 26C.

1) On Monday, Wednesday, and Friday I take the bus to work. _____

2) I'm going to Taiwan because I'd like to open a language school there. _____

3) The mayor said terrible things about the police chief when she learned about the bribe. _____

4) Her son got a little wild, but she acted immediately to correct his behavior. _____

5) We'll have to get a new roof pretty soon. _____

6) When my daughter was 14, she was almost impossible to control. _____

7) Old Uncle Fudd has been crazy now for a couple of years. _____

8) He'll lie and she'll swear to it. They're a lot like each other. _____

9) You should have that cut treated. _____

10) "Can I borrow your bike?" "Well, OK." _____

The Idiom Book

Lesson 27
SHAKESPEARE FESTIVAL

27A. Read.

Peg: Are we going to take in the Shakespeare Festival this month?

Pat: <u>I'm afraid</u> it's <u>out of the question</u> this month.

Peg: Are we <u>running short of</u> dough?

Pat: Of time. We have to <u>go all out</u> this month at work on a big project.

Peg: Well, <u>first things first</u>. You do have to <u>make a living</u>.

Pat: <u>Keep your chin up</u>. Maybe we can get to *Macbeth* in August.

Peg: <u>Keep your fingers crossed</u>. Oh, <u>by the way</u>, does your mother plan to go with us, if we go?

Pat: <u>I'm afraid so</u>.

27B. Read and fill in the blanks.

SPEEDWELL PRODUCTS
23 South Market Street
East Berlin, PA

From: Robert W. Johnson   Date: August 23
To: Arnold Glick
Re: Your employment with Speedwell

    Arnold, this is a hard letter to write, but following up on our conversation yesterday, <u>afraid</u> your job here is ended, temporarily. We're <u>running</u> <u>of</u> business orders, and so using any non-family workers is simply <u>out</u> <u>the question</u>. I know that you have to <u>a living</u>, and you're a good worker. We're <u>going</u> <u>out</u> to get new business and we'd like to rehire you as soon as we can, but we have to put <u>first</u> <u>first</u>. I know you understand.
    <u>By</u> <u>way</u>, you asked yesterday if you'd lose your health insurance if you lost your job; well, I'm <u>so</u>. But <u>keep your</u> <u>up</u>, and <u>keep your</u> <u>crossed</u>; business should improve soon.

54   The Idiom Book

27C. Matching Exercise. In the parentheses write the letter of the meaning for each idiom.

Idiom

1) run short of ( )
2) out of the question ( )
3) I'm afraid ( )
4) go all out ( )
5) first things first ( )
6) by the way ( )
7) I'm afraid so ( )
8) keep your fingers crossed ( )
9) make a living ( )
10) keep your chin up ( )

Meaning

(a) to work or try as hard as possible
(b) to use or spend almost all of something
(c) impossible
(d) regrettably
(e) hope for good luck
(f) oh, incidentally,
(g) yes, unfortunately
(h) stay cheerful
(i) to earn enough money to survive
(j) [do] the most important things first

27D. Change each of the following sentences with an idiom from 27C.

1) Regrettably, we have to leave now. _____

2) Buying a new car is impossible this year. _____

3) I don't have much patience left—you'd better behave! _____

4) This election is really important. We have to try as hard as possible. _____

5) The first things we have to ensure are the most important ones: food and shelter. _____

6) She can't even earn enough to survive at that job. _____

7) Don't be discouraged—you'll find a better job. _____

8) Wish for good luck. Maybe we can still get to the airport on time. _____

9) Here're your keys. Oh, incidentally, your car's almost out of gas. _____

10) "Is that my blind date?" "Yes, unfortunately." _____

Lesson 28

POSSIBLE

28A. Read.

Ellen: Well, Mr. Sharp's offer is <u>on the table</u>. He told me frankly that we can <u>take it or leave it</u>; there'll be no <u>give and take</u> <u>on his part</u>.

Alfred: Hmm, pretty blunt. You think he's <u>out to</u> <u>take us to the cleaners</u>?

Ellen: No, I don't. I *do* think he's <u>all business</u> and not very good at <u>small talk</u>.

Alfred: Well, I'm <u>having second thoughts</u> about the wisdom of sharing our business with him.

Ellen: Oh, <u>get a grip</u>. His bluntness is just honesty. I trust him.

28B. Read and fill in the blanks.

From: Helen Jacobs <HelensProducts@flashnet.com>
Date: September 20
To: Lance Bergstrom <Beautyworks@Superonline.com>
Subject: My Final Offer

Lance,

My proposal to you is <u>the table—take it</u> leave it. There'll be no _____ <u>and take on my</u> _____. You can't see it, but that other offer from Verna is dangerous. She is of course very good at intimate <u>small</u> _____, especially with men who have money. However, she is _____ <u>business</u>. I'm sure she's _____ <u>to take you</u> _____ <u>the cleaners</u>. If within the next couple of weeks you <u>have</u> _____ <u>thoughts</u> about what you're doing, write me a note. All I can say to you right now is: <u>get a</u> _____.

Or you'll be sorry.

Helen

BUSINESS MERGER

28C. Matching Exercise. In the parentheses write the letter of the meaning for each idiom.

Idiom

1) give and take ( )
2) take it or leave it ( )
3) on the table ( )
4) on one's part ( )
5) have second thoughts ( )
6) take someone to the cleaners ( )
7) get a grip ( )
8) small talk ( )
9) out to ( )
10) all business ( )

Meaning

(a) from someone [describes how someone feels or thinks]
(b) compromise
(c) either accept or reject something with no discussion
(d) open to discussion, acceptance, or rejection
(e) relaxed, casual conversation or chat
(f) to become less certain about something
(g) don't be so sensitive or impulsive; control yourself
(h) interested only in business/work
(i) determined (to do something)
(j) to get or win all of someone's money, often dishonestly

28D. Change each of the following sentences with an idiom from 28C.

1) The question is now open to discussion by the committee. _____

2) If you want the car, you buy it as is. I'm not going to bargain or haggle. _____

3) Hmm. You don't believe in compromise, do you? _____

4) There'll be no concessions from him. _____

5) I believe that Bloatmart is determined to destroy the small hardware stores. _____

6) Boy, my "friends" won all my money at the game last night. _____

7) Mr. Sharp has no time for fun; he's always thinking about work. _____

8) He finds it very hard to have a relaxed, friendly chat with anyone. All he can talk about is work. ___

9) You know, I'm not so sure about my trip to China right now. Maybe I'll delay it by a couple of months. _____

10) So she made a remark about your dress: don't be so sensitive—who cares what she says? _____

The Idiom Book 57

Lesson 29

BIG GUNS

29A. Read.

Bud: What's <u>on the docket</u> for this morning?

Pam: The <u>big guns</u> are coming in from New York. <u>I'm to</u> <u>bring them up to date</u> on our operations here.

Bud: The president's <u>nobody's fool</u>, so <u>watch your step</u>.

Pam: Oh, she and I <u>go back a long way</u>—we always <u>play it straight</u> with each other. But you're right—you've got to be <u>on your toes</u> with her.

Bud: I guess this morning's business will be <u>a piece of cake</u> for you.

29B. Read and fill in the blanks.

Memo

To: All dept. chiefs   Date: February 24
From: Vice President Woodson

    The _____<u>gun</u> is coming in from NYC tomorrow morning, and he'll probably be here three days. There's nothing official _____ <u>the docket</u> re the visit, but he emailed me that he wants to meet you all, individually. <u>I'm</u>___ <u>bring him up to</u>_____ on the progress of the coal-nuclear conversion. If he should ask any of you about that, and of course he will, let me tell you this: he and I <u>go</u>_____<u>a long way</u>, and you'd better be<u> on your</u>_____ when he questions you; he's <u>nobody's</u>_____. _____<u>your step</u> with him; he <u>plays</u>_____<u>straight</u> and expects his employees to do the same. He's actually one of the most decent men I've ever known, but your meeting with him won't be <u>a piece</u>_____<u>cake</u>.

---

58   The Idiom Book

29C. Matching Exercise. In the parentheses write the letter of the meaning for each idiom.

Idiom

1) bring someone up to date ( )
2) be to ( )
3) on the docket ( )
4) big gun ( )
5) play it straight ( )
6) watch your step ( )
7) go back a long way ( )
8) a piece of cake ( )
9) on your toes ( )
10) nobody's fool ( )

Meaning

(a) to give someone the latest information and news
(b) be required or expected to
(c) a leader, or boss
(d) scheduled or planned
(e) to be open and honest; not try to trick someone
(f) alert and ready for anything that happens
(g) something that's easy to do
(h) have known each other for a long time
(i) be careful
(j) someone who is hard to trick or deceive

29D. Change each of the following sentences with an idiom from 29C.

1) Please ask the administrative assistant what we have scheduled for this afternoon. _____

2) The president of the whole outfit's arriving for an inspection tomorrow morning. _____

3) We have to be here at 0700 tomorrow. _____

4) Have a seat. I'll give you the latest scoop about what's happening in the office. _____

5) She's no dummy—don't even think about trying to fool her. _____

6) Be careful in the basement: it's easy to trip and fall down there. _____

7) Those two have known each other for 20 years. _____

8) Tell the cops the truth—they'll find out anyway. _____

9) Listen: this is a delicate and somewhat dangerous situation, so be ready for anything. _____

10) Winning the election was very easy. I was the only candidate. _____

The Idiom Book 59

Lesson 30

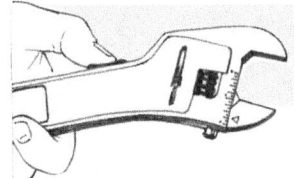

CAR REPAIR

30A. Read.

Ali: Hey there, Hidei. What are you doing? Something wrong with the car?

Hidei: Oh, hi, Ali. Yeah, the old car <u>broke down</u> again. I have to replace my alternator and I'm <u>at a loss as to</u> how to begin.

Ali: Let me <u>give you a hand</u>. If you've got the part here, we can <u>get it over with</u> in a couple of hours.

Hidei: Great. Could we <u>get at it</u> right now?

Ali: <u>Sure thing</u>. The first thing you do is set everything electrical to "off," then disconnect the negative battery cable and put it well away from the battery post <u>so that</u> we don't short anything.

[Later]

Hidei: <u>Thank goodness</u> you came by, Ali. <u>Had it not been for</u> you, I couldn't have done it.

30B. Read and fill in the blanks.

> To: Mr. John B. Strickland, CEO <JBStricklandCEO@CBC.com>
> From: Veronica Halper, Personnel <VeronicaH@CBC.com>
> Subject: Problem at CBC South
>
>   Mr. Strickland, you sent me here to determine the cause of the factory labor-management dispute at CBC South, and after my first day here, I was <u>at   loss as</u> why the talks <u>broke</u> again. Both sides seemed suspicious of me and no one was willing to <u>give me a</u> defining the problem <u>so</u> I could <u>get   it</u>.
>   Well, I asked a shop steward this morning if she could help me understand what was happening, and she immediately said, "<u>Sure</u>," and helped me get to the heart of the matter. It seems that it's factory policy that the machine operators have to ask permission—like little kids—to go to the toilet! <u>Thank</u> for that steward. <u>Had it not for</u> her, I'd still be wondering. All I have left to do is to tell management to scrap that counterproductive policy. I'm going to <u>get that with</u> before lunch, and hop the afternoon flight back. I'll give you a full report upon my return.
>
>   Ms. Halper

30C. Matching Exercise. In the parentheses write the letter of the meaning for each idiom.

Idiom

1) as to ( )
2) break down ( )
3) give someone a hand ( )
4) at a loss ( )
5) thank goodness ( )
6) had it not been for ( )
7) sure thing ( )
8) so that ( )
9) get it over with ( )
10) get at it ( )

Meaning

(a) to help someone
(b) about; concerning
(c) unsure; puzzled
(d) stop, fall apart, fail to progress
(e) for this purpose:
(f) I'm very glad and grateful
(g) without [in past time]
(h) of course
(i) begin (an activity or task)
(j) to finish (an activity or task)

30D. Change each of the following sentences with an idiom from 30C.

1) Mike's truck unfortunately stopped right in the middle of the bridge. _____

2) I'm puzzled about why she left so suddenly. [Two idioms.] _____

3) Could you help me with this crate? _____

4) I have to fire her today, and I want to finish that job right now. _____

5) We've got a lot of snow to clear, so let's start. _____

6) "Could you help me get this load on the truck?" "Of course." _____

7) Have the two groups meet once a week. The point is that they continue to talk to each other. _____

8) I'm glad the rain stopped. _____

9) Without that break in the weather, we'd have got lost on the mountain. _____

The Idiom Book

Lesson 31
HOUSE MAINTENANCE

31A. Read.

Pat: I <u>don't think much of</u> the paint job your brother did on this house. I need someone to <u>lend me a hand</u> getting together paint, primer, thinner, tarp, ladder, scraper, wire brush, <u>and so on</u>.

Peg: What's <u>on your mind</u>? Repainting the whole house?

Pat: No, just the windows, <u>for starters</u>.

Peg: OK. <u>Aside from</u> paint and primer, I think we already have all the things you named.

Pat: Man, an old wooden house keeps the owner <u>on the go</u>.

Peg: It sure does. It's hard enough to <u>keep up with</u> all the maintenance <u>much less</u> <u>set aside</u> the money for it.

31B. Read and fill in the blanks.

From: Terri Smoltz <Tsmoltz@DailyReview.com>
To: Martha Nestor <Nestorfamily@hometel.com>
Date: June 30
Subject: Working at the Review

Dear Mom,

   Apparently the editor <u>doesn't think</u> _____ <u>of</u> my writing. <u>For</u> _____ , he said my piece on the police commission was wordy, overblown, <u>and</u> _____ <u>on</u>. He's offered to <u>lend me a</u> _____ at pruning it, but I think he may have something other than pruning _____ <u>his mind</u>. Someone left a help-wanted section of the paper on my desk.

   And he keeps me <u>on the</u> _____ with really insulting minor assignments: obits, school lunches, etc. He makes me proofread—not copyedit—the sports pages. I think he believes my proper role is staying home and <u>keeping</u> _____ <u>with</u> the housework while my husband earns the family income. I'm afraid the work here isn't very interesting, <u>much</u> _____ important. But <u>aside</u> _____ those minor matters, things are fine here, and I have set aside enough for a trip back to Montana this summer.

Love to Pop

Terri

62 The Idiom Book

31C. Matching Exercise. In the parentheses write the letter of the meaning for each idiom.

Idiom

1) and so on ( )
2) lend someone a hand ( )
3) not think much of (something) ( )
4) on someone's mind ( )
5) much less ( )
6) keep up with ( )
7) on the go ( )
8) aside from ( )
9) for starters ( )
10) set aside ( )

Meaning

(a) in one's thoughts; what one is thinking
(b) and similar things
(c) to help someone
(d) think that something is not very good
(e) maintain
(f) save; hold for later
(g) also; too; besides
(h) very busy
(i) except for; besides
(j) [1] at the beginning [2] as one reason . . .

31D. Change each of the following sentences with an idiom from 31C.

1) She didn't think that was a very good movie. _____

2) Could somebody help me with this luggage? _____

3) She loves toy cars, trucks, tractors, planes, trains, and things like that. _____

4) The idea of emigrating has been in my thoughts for the last four years. _____

5) I'm going to remodel the garage, and at the start I'm going to change the doors. _____

6) There's nothing left to do besides putting the tools away. _____

7) With four kids, they're always busy. _____

8) I'm just barely staying on top of all my work. _____

9) He can't work amicably with family members, and certainly not strangers. _____

10) We have saved a thousand dollars for a new car. _____

The Idiom Book   63

Lesson 32
A JOB IN TORONTO

32A. Read.

Betsy: You were <u>down in the dumps</u> and <u>on edge</u> for months, and now you're cheerful again. What's happened?

Fred: Well, I got a call a couple of hours ago that I've got the Toronto job, <u>provided that</u> I can start the first of the month.

Betsy: So we're <u>pulling up stakes</u> again.

Fred: Yeah, but I know you'll <u>take it in stride</u>. And we'll <u>put down roots</u> there within a year.

Betsy: I guess I'd better <u>let Mom in on</u> this. You sure you're not <u>jumping the gun</u>?

Fred: Yes, I am. She made me a formal offer on the phone, and she's going to put a written confirmation in the mail today. Your mom will be <u>all for</u> it—she loves Toronto. And as you know, the move will be good for my career <u>in the long run</u>.

32B. Read and fill in the blanks.

> To: Lola Roth <lolaro@supernet.com>
> Date: August 23
> From: Barbara Finnegan <barbf250@wahoo.com>
> Subject: Taipei!
>
> Dear Lola,
>   I know that you've been <u>down</u> the dumps because of the layoff, and I've been <u>edge</u> waiting to hear about the Taiwan job; now I can <u>let you in</u> something I got on the phone a few hours ago: they've offered me the Taipei slot, <u>that</u> I can get there by the middle of August. I assume you'll be <u>all</u> it. It of course means <u>pulling stakes</u> and trying to <u>down roots</u> in a new, exotic culture, but I know you'll <u>everything right in stride</u>. And <u>in the</u> run it'll be good for my career. And I'm sure you can find a job teaching English.
>   I've already called the real estate woman. Am I <u>jumping the</u>?
>   Barb

64 The Idiom Book

32C. Matching Exercise. In the parentheses write the letter of the meaning for each idiom.

Idiom

1) on edge ( )
2) provided that ( )
3) pull up stakes ( )
4) down in the dumps ( )
5) in the long run ( )
6) put down roots ( )
7) let someone in on ( )
8) jump the gun ( )
9) all for ( )
10) take (it) in stride ( )

Meaning

(a) to leave home and move to a new one
(b) if
(c) nervous; jumpy
(d) dejected; depressed
(e) to do something too soon
(f) happy or enthusiastic about something
(g) eventually
(h) to tell someone about something
(i) to settle somewhere and establish a home
(j) to not let something upset or stop you

32D. Change each of the following sentences with an idiom from 32C.

1) She's been dejected since her dog died. _____

2) Ali seems nervous and jumpy. I wonder what's bothering him. _____

3) Yes, you can have the afternoon off, if you finish the work this weekend. _____

4) My parents have sold their house, so they'll be moving again. _____

5) My mom doesn't let their moves bother her too much. _____

6) They get established pretty fast in new neighborhoods. _____

7) I wish you'd tell me what the hell's happening. _____

8) They should have waited a bit before accepting that first offer: they got a better one a day after they agreed to it. _____

9) Sure, I'd be glad to see new management here. _____

10) Eventually, these moves will have helped your career. _____

Lesson 33

LONG TIME NO SEE

33A. Read.

Howie: So how was the reunion?

Rob: They hadn't seen each other in three years and they were all <u>a tad</u> too polite.

Howie: Did Minnie give her dad <u>the cold shoulder</u>?

Rob: No. They clutched each other awkwardly, and that <u>broke the ice</u>.

Howie: I'll bet Cookie greeted Grandpa with genuine affection and that <u>made his day</u>.

Rob: Oh, yes, bless her. <u>Picking up where you leave off</u> isn't always easy, whether with a grandparent or an <u>old flame</u>. But Cookie did it. And a long-lost relative can be a <u>pain in the ass</u>, especially if he's the kind who likes to <u>dish dirt</u>, and Gramps did manage to <u>let slip</u> something about Cookie's <u>old flame</u>, Carl Zamaro.

Howie: Yeah, If you see certain relatives just <u>once in a while</u>, that's often enough.

33B. Read and fill in the blanks.

To: Sapphire Diamond <sapphire@hotcast.com>
Date: November 14
From: Rock <RockRobinson@moonnet.com>

Dear Sapphire,

   Why did you give me <u>the   shoulder</u> the other night at the dance after you first <u>made   day</u> by giving me that wonderful smile when I walked in? Was it perhaps because I seemed to you <u> tad</u> too friendly to Opal? She didn't know anybody there, and I was only trying to <u>break   ice</u> for her and make her feel comfortable.

   Can't we <u>pick   where we left</u> off last week? Can't you pretend I'm an <u>old   </u> instead of a current <u>pain in the   </u>? <u>Dish   </u> about Opal with your friends all you want—I don't care.

   <u>Once   a while</u>, when I'm in a late-night talk with my old pals, I realize that I <u> slip</u> that you're the woman who matters to me. Forgive me?

Rock

33C. Matching Exercise. In the parentheses write the letter of the meaning for each idiom.

Idiom

1) a tad ( )
2) give someone the cold shoulder ( )
3) make someone's day ( )
4) break the ice ( )
5) pick up where you left off ( )
6) let slip ( )
7) pain in the ass ( )
8) dish dirt ( )
9) old flame ( )
10) once in a while ( )

Meaning

(a) to please someone a lot
(b) to make a situation less tense and more relaxed
(c) to be unfriendly to someone
(d) to a small extent; a little
(e) to gossip about someone
(f) to tell something inadvertently
(g) occasionally; not often
(h) a person who's an annoyance, or nuisance
(i) a former sweetheart
(j) begin where you stopped before

33D. Change each of the following sentences with an idiom from 33C.

1) "How's the patient?" "He's better to some extent, but not much." _____

2) When Sapphire saw Rock at the meeting, she gave him a very unfriendly reception. _____

3) Even though the chairman's joke was pretty lame, it let everybody relax nicely. _____

4) When Cookie won the race it really pleased us. _____

5) "The meeting will please come to order. Let's try to start where we stopped last week." ____

6) When I was getting off the A train at 14th street, I literally bumped into a former sweetheart of mine. _____

7) My brother-in-law is a nuisance. He can't keep a job. _____

8) Aunt Mabel and Aunt Tillie love to gossip about the flashy woman across the street._____

9) The reporter got into trouble because she accidentally revealed the name of a confidential source. _____

10) She thinks of him occasionally._____

Lesson 34
TECHNICAL TRAINING

34A. Read.

Ray: <u>What the hell</u> is a "URL"?

David: "Universal Resource Locator"—an email address, I think. The computer geeks' English <u>could stand</u> some polishing.

Ray: Amen. I finally <u>got the feel of</u> my word processor mostly <u>by trial and error</u>, and not by using any manual.

David: Uh-huh. But before that happened with me, trying to understand the dope in "Help" almost drove me <u>over the edge</u>.

Ray: It drove me <u>up the wall</u>.

David: Learning to use a processor isn't <u>all fun and games</u>, but the device does make it possible to write faster. No more tearing a page out of the typewriter and redoing the whole thing.

Ray: Granted. You can now correct a mistake <u>on the spot</u>, in one thirtieth the time. But <u>the jury is still out on</u> whether the quality of the writing has improved <u>along with</u> the speed.

34B. Read and fill in the blanks.

Journal entry for September 29

Re: Grimm

I wonder <u>what</u> _____ hell's wrong with Grimm. He fired a machine operator who he said couldn't <u>get the</u> _____ of his grinder. He <u>could</u> _____ some training in how to run a machine shop. He knows that you learn to run one of those machines gradually, <u>by trial</u> _____ error. It takes time—there's no other way. It isn't <u>all</u> _____ and games working with Grimm. Trying to reason with the guy drives me _____ <u>the wall</u>. And it drives me _____ <u>the edge</u> to try to explain to the operators his screwy shop regulations. If I owned this shop, I'd fire him <u>on</u> _____ spot, <u>along</u> _____ that stupid assistant of his. And <u>the jury's</u> _____ <u>out on</u> whether the used grinder he bought is any good.

68 The Idiom Book

34C. Matching Exercise. In the parentheses write the letter of the meaning for each idiom.

Idiom   *Meaning*

1) could stand (   )   (a) trying until you find the right way or method
2) what the hell (   )   (b) to learn gradually how to do something
3) get the feel of (   )   (c) to need or want something
4) trial and error (   )   (d) What!? [Angrily]
5) along with (   )   (e) immediately
6) drive someone up the wall (   )   (f) it's still unknown
7) the jury's still out on (   )   (g) at the same time as; together with
8) on the spot (   )   (h) simply casual pleasure
9) all fun and games (   )   (i) to annoy or irritate someone greatly
10) drive someone over the edge (   )   (j) to make someone insane or crazy

34D. Change each of the following sentences with an idiom from 34C.

1) What happened!? Why is there broken glass on the floor? _____

2) I need a few days off. _____
3) Does Cookie handle the car pretty well now? _____
4) I finally learned how to use the word processor by trying and trying until I got it right. ____

5) Her leaving him actually drove him crazy. _____
6) That guy's constant chatter is intensely irritating. _____

7) Dealing with my in-laws isn't always a simple pleasure. _____

8) When they got a look at her, they immediately offered her the role. _____

9) We still don't know if she can do the job as director. _____

10) He got promoted at the same time as the other two. _____

The Idiom Book 69

Lesson 35
ROUGHING IT

35A. Read.

Pat: Here we are at Backwoods Campground! We'll be <u>roughing it</u> here.

Peg: <u>How so</u>?

Pat: The toilets are <u>quite a way</u> from the campsite.

Peg: Well that's <u>a hell of a note</u>!

Pat: It won't kill us to <u>hoof it</u>.

Peg: I <u>could do without</u> the inconvenience. I really prefer a motel.

Pat: Nonsense—you can <u>take it</u>. We'll only be here two nights, so don't <u>lose it</u>.

Peg: OK, I'll <u>keep my cool</u>. I'll be <u>on my best behavior</u>, just for you.

35B. Read and fill in the blanks.

Journal Entry for August 23

We just got back from our trip out west, "<u>roughing</u>   " and I was remembering how once Pop and I were camping in the Green Mountains near Jay Peak and I commented that we were "roughing it." Pop grinned and said, "<u>How</u>   ?" When I explained it was because we had to <u>hoof</u>   to the latrine, which was <u>quite</u>   way away, he replied that you rough it when your latrine is behind a shrub. If there is a shrub. But, he said, you learn how to <u>take</u>   , and that builds character. Hmm.

   Pop taught me to be <u>on my</u>   behavior when out hiking—to leave nothing but tracks. Recently, however, I learned that our old campsite is overwhelmed with ATV users. That's <u>a hell of a</u>   and I <u>could do</u>   those ATVs. But I don't <u>lose</u>   any more when I meet a gang of them. <u>I keep</u>   cool. They're just people who love the woods AND their big, ugly noisy toys.

70   The Idiom Book

35C. Matching Exercise. In the parentheses write the letter of the meaning for each idiom.

Idiom

1) how so ( )
2) rough it ( )
3) a hell of a note ( )
4) quite a way ( )
5) keep one's cool ( )
6) could do without ( )
7) lose it ( )
8) take it ( )
9) hoof it ( )
10) on one's best behavior ( )

Meaning

(a) a disagreeable surprise
(b) pretty far
(c) please explain
(d) to be without the usual comforts and conveniences
(e) to get upset or angry
(f) to stay calm; not become upset or angry
(g) very polite and considerate
(h) endure something bad or unpleasant
(i) don't like
(j) to walk

35D. Change each of the following sentences with an idiom from 35C.

1) When you camp in the hills, you live very simply. There're no conveniences. _____

2) "Her letter explains the whole thing." "Oh? Please explain." _____

3) It's pretty far to the next gas station. _____

4) She just quit? Well that's a nasty surprise! _____

5) The car's out of gas so we'll have to walk. _____

6) I don't like the TV in the living room. _____

7) It's pretty cold here in the winter, but you'll learn to endure it. _____

8) I wish you wouldn't get so mad when you hear that guy on the radio. _____

9) Try to stay calm when you hear him telling his lies. _____

10) The kids all behaved like angels for Grandma. _____

The Idiom Book

Lesson 36

THE ENGLISH

36A. Read.

Good morning, class. Today we'll begin with a brief look at the history of English.

The English language <u>took shape</u> in Great Britain in the Dark Ages, when marauders from what is now Denmark and North Germany invaded and eventually conquered the Island. The marauders, who <u>went by the names of</u> Angles, Saxons, and Jutes, were some of the forebears of Vikings. Their various dialects coalesced and <u>took root</u> in Britain and became a separate Germanic tongue, now a sister language to modern Danish, Dutch, German, Icelandic, Norwegian, and Swedish.

In AD 1066, descendants of Vikings who had settled in Normandy invaded and conquered England and settled there <u>for good</u>. Those conquerors <u>set in motion</u> their own system of laws and used only the French language in all the government and legal affairs of England. But English again became the dominant language of England in the 14th century, and it now <u>holds linguistic sway</u> in more parts of the world than any other language. <u>Chances are</u> it will retain its status for <u>some time</u>.

A Glasgow dockworker and his counterpart from Cape Town can now <u>chew the fat</u> in English, and bridge players from Newfoundland and New South Wales can <u>match wits</u> on the Net in their native language.

36B. Read and fill in the blanks.

```
                    TOP SECRET
              DESTROY AFTER READING

Dear fellow patriots,
    Our resistance movement is _____ shape; but for security reasons, we'll go____the
name of "Hope Advertising." The determination to resist took_____ when the authorities
closed all the opposition newspapers ____good and set in_____ the protests that have
become the resistance. Chances_____ this present climate of fear and conformity will
_____ sway for some_____, so be very careful to talk of the weather or other such trivia
when you're chewing_____ fat with someone in a coffee shop: you're matching_____ with
rich, powerful, well-organized, and determined fascists.
    Don't lose hope.
    X
```

72 The Idiom Book

LANGUAGE

36C. Matching Exercise. In the parentheses write the letter of the meaning for each idiom.

Idiom

1) take root ( )
2) go by the name of ( )
3) take shape ( )
4) for good ( )
5) chances are ( )
6) hold sway ( )
7) set in motion ( )
8) some time ( )
9) chew the fat ( )
10) match wits ( )

Meaning

(a) permanently
(b) to become established; grow
(c) to be called; have the name of
(d) to form, or develop
(e) a rather long time
(f) to chat casually
(g) to compete intellectually
(h) it is probable that; probably
(i) to dominate something
(j) [1] to establish [2] to cause, or create

36D. Change each of the following sentences with an idiom from 36C.

1) Our garden is developing nicely. _____
2) That, folks, was the 1950s band called "The Marshmallow Strings." _____
3) The resistance to the regime is growing. _____
4) I'm off cigarettes permanently! _____
5) Those anti-smoking regulations are now official and binding. _____
6) The classical genre no longer dominates serious music as it once did. _____
7) Don't worry—you'll probably get the job. _____
8) I've been waiting to see the doctor for rather a long time now. _____
9) Jake and Art are just drinking coffee and chatting casually. _____
10) When those two chess players compete, they get worldwide attention. _____

The Idiom Book

Lesson 37

FIELD BOTANY

37A. Read.

Cindy: How can you <u>tell</u> all these trees <u>apart</u>?

Carmen: I <u>make use of</u> the pictures and descriptions in my manual of trees and shrubs.

Cindy: I <u>get it</u>. All you need is the manual.

Carmen: Well, let's look at a maple and an ash. <u>That way</u>, you'll <u>get a handle on</u> how to proceed.

Cindy: Why those two <u>in particular</u>?

Carmen: Because they're very easy to identify. If you want to get your jacket, we can <u>take a whack at</u> it now.

Cindy: OK. <u>You can't beat</u> the woods here in the fall.

Carmen: Yeah. My dad and I spent a lot of time <u>tramping around</u> in the woods when I was just a youngster and I've loved them <u>ever since</u>.

37B. Read and fill in the blanks.

> From: Harry Adams <harryadams 250@SMN.com>
> Date: Thursday, July 5
> To: Ruby Okuna <RandKokuna@ Syncast.com>
> Subject: Berries
>
> Ruby,
>
> If you want to <u>take a</u> _____ <u>at getting</u> _____ <u>handle on</u> how and where to (and where not to) <u>make</u> _____ <u>of</u> your new "Illustrated Flora," come out with me Sunday morning; I'll show you where to look for blueberries, huckleberries, wintergreen berries, and wild strawberries. And I'll show you how to <u>tell</u> huckleberries and blueberries _____. My dad showed me how to hunt and find those things when we spent our summers <u>tramping</u> _____ in the Maine woods, and I've been doing it for fun _____ <u>since</u>.
>
> Heck, I'll tell you about the hucks and the blues right now: the huckleberry leaves have tiny yellow dots, sometimes on both sides—and the blueberries don't. I didn't <u>get</u> _____ about the dots until he showed me with a lens, so bring a 10-power lens Sunday, if you have one, and if you decide to come.
>
> As you know, <u>you</u> _____ <u>beat</u> the scent of these northern woods in the fall, and __ <u>particular</u> the smell of sassafras, sweetfern, and the broken twigs of the yellow and the black birch. I'll show you all those.
>
> And if you come, drive your car over here and we'll go on in mine from here. _____ <u>way</u>, you can give your old junk a rest.
>
> Harry

74 The Idiom Book

37C. Matching Exercise. In the parentheses write the letter of the meaning for each idiom.

Idiom

1) get it ( )
2) make use of ( )
3) tell apart ( )
4) that way ( )
5) ever since ( )
6) in particular ( )
7) take a whack at ( )
8) tramp around ( )
9) you can't beat ( )
10) get a handle on ( )

Meaning

(a) by doing that
(b) to understand
(c) to utilize, or use something
(d) to distinguish things that are similar or alike
(e) there is nothing better than. . . .
(f) walk in the woods
(g) continuously, from that time
(h) to try to do something
(i) especially; specifically
(j) to begin to understand something

37D. Change each of the following sentences with an idiom from 37C.

1) He still can't distinguish a spruce from a fir. _____

2) To check the alternator I follow the procedure outlined in the manual. _____

3) Now I understand: I check the reading and then reconnect the regulator. _____

4) Follow the procedure exactly. By doing that, you won't ruin any electronic components. ___

5) I'm starting to get pretty good at pulling the mower blade, sharpening it, and reinstalling it.

6) Out of the whole class, why did you pick those two kids especially? _____

7) Snowboarding? I've never done it, but I'd like to try it. _____

8) There's nothing better than Vermont in October. _____

9) I used to spend hours walking everywhere in the woods behind my house. _____

10) And always, from that time, I've loved winter. _____

The Idiom Book 75

Lesson 38
TAKING A CHANCE

38A. Read.

Steve: When Tom's girl <u>gave him the heave-ho</u>, he went out and <u>tied one on</u>.

Dick: Well, he was <u>pushing his luck</u>; he never stopped <u>playing the field</u>, and he's <u>gone and</u> done it this time.

Steve: That's <u>too bad</u>. I think he really loves her.

Dick: Nah, he's always <u>on the make</u>. I think she was right to <u>give him his walking papers</u>. Anyway, romance is always a <u>crapshoot</u>. Speaking of which, I think that beautiful woman over there might <u>have designs on me</u>!

Steve: Dreamer!

38B. Read and fill in the blanks.

> From: Sven Lindstrom<SL@Protodyne.com>
> Date: Friday, May 25
> To: Daisy Miller <dmiller@Smithco.com>
> Subject: Our old boss
>
> Hi Daisy,
>
>   Mr. Cash (remember him) <u>got</u> _____ <u>heave-ho</u> this morning, so he went out and <u>tied one</u> _____ down at McSorley's Bar. He <u>was pushing his</u> _____ with his drinking problem, and now he has <u>gone</u> _____ lost his job because of it. It's <u>too</u> _____, because he's got three kids. Despite his "family-man" status, though, he was always _____ <u>the make</u> here in the office. But they <u>gave him</u> _____ <u>walking papers</u> because of his drinking, not his womanizing.
>   A lot of young men now are like him; they keep _____ <u>the field</u> after they're engaged, and sometimes even after they're married.
>   But I certainly don't say that romance is a _____ <u>shoot</u> for everybody—I hope and trust you still <u>have</u> _____ <u>on me</u>!
>
>   Sven

The Idiom Book

ON LOVE

38C. Matching Exercise. In the parentheses write the letter of the meaning for each idiom.

Idiom

1) tie one on ( )
2) give (someone) the heave-ho ( )
3) push one's luck ( )
4) play the field ( )
5) on the make ( )
6) too bad ( )
7) go and ( )
8) have designs on (someone) ( )
9) crapshoot ( )
10) give someone walking papers ( )

Meanimg

(a) to date a lot of different people
(b) to deserve, or invite (something bad)
(c) to get drunk
(d) to dismiss someone from a job or a personal relationship
(e) to dismiss someone
(f) a risky gamble
(g) to want to have a relationship with a specific person
(h) eager for sex with anyone
(i) regrettable; unfortunate
(j) impetuously and foolishly; wrongly or mistakenly

38D. Change each of the following sentences with an idiom from 38C.

1) Pearl told Jim she didn't want to date him anymore. _____

2) Cynthia got drunk at the reception. _____

3) She got demoted because she just refused to work very hard and didn't try to do better. _____

4) He dates a lot of different girls. _____

5) She foolishly married that silly musician. _____

6) He resigned, and that's unfortunate. They liked his work. _____

7) He tries to go out with every attractive woman he meets. _____

8) The director just fired the sales manager. _____

9) Driving a long way in the winter is always a gamble. _____

10) He wanted her as soon as he saw her. _____

Lesson 39
PRAISE & THANKS

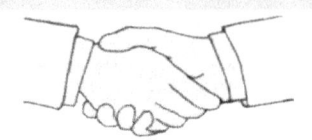

39A. Read.

Beth: The recipe for my scalloped potatoes has long been <u>in demand</u>, so here it is.

Andrea: Did you <u>by chance</u> learn it from Grandma?

Beth: I'm not <u>at liberty</u> to divulge the source. <u>At any rate</u>, please let me continue.

Andrea: <u>By all means</u>.

Beth: You<u>'ve got to</u> cut the potatoes into sixteenth-of-an-inch slices.

Andrea: <u>How the devil</u> can you get them that thin?

Beth: I've got a German hand slicer that does it <u>in nothing flat</u>.

Andrea: I have to <u>hand it to</u> you; you're occasionally <u>of use</u> around the kitchen.

39B. Read and fill in the blanks.

From: Thomas Lorenzo <Tom@Wildlifeprotectors.org>
Date: Thursday, October 25
To: Sylvia French <Sylvia@EarthSave.org>
Subject: Marci Hassan

Sylvia,

    You were right. Your young techie, Marci, is great. I've *got* _hand_ *to* her—she found and destroyed that computer virus *in nothing* _____. I wish I could understand *how* _devil_ she did it; I asked her, but she said, of course, that she wasn't *at* _____ to tell me. I can see why she's ___*demand*___ ; would you ___*chance*___ consider lending her services to us for about six months? I suppose you can't, but, *at* _rate_, thanks again and ___*all means*___ call me if I can be *of* _____ to you in any way. I really owe you.

                                                          Tom

39C. Matching Exercise. In the parentheses write the letter of the meaning for each idiom.

Idiom

1) at any rate ( )
2) by chance ( )
3) at liberty ( )
4) in demand ( )
5) by all means ( )
6) have got to ( )
7) how the devil ( )
8) in nothing flat ( )
9) hand it to someone ( )
10) of use ( )

Meaning

(a) [1] but I want to talk more: [2] regardless
(b) permitted or allowed (to do something)
(c) perhaps; possibly
(d) popular
(d) almost instantly
(e) congratulate
(f) useful; helpful
(g) How!? [quite surprised]
(h) must; have to
(i) of course

39D. Change each of the following sentences with an idiom from 39C.

1) Cell phones are really popular now. _____
2) Have you perhaps found a set of keys? _____
3) I'm not allowed to tell you the source's name. _____
4) She may have to work tonight but, regardless, I'm going to the concert. _____
5) Borrow my car? Of course. Any time. _____
6) By terms of the treaty, we're obliged to grant them entry visas for 30 days. _____
7) How did you do that so fast!? _____
8) She found the problem with the printer almost immediately. _____
9) I really must congratulate you. That was a smooth performance. _____
10) I hope you find the manual helpful in your work. _____

The Idiom Book 79

Lesson 40
EAST MICHIGAN TO

40A. Read.

Peg: If we're <u>on the road</u> by 4:30 tomorrow morning, we should be in Springfield <u>in time</u> for supper.

Pat: The bags are <u>all set</u>; they're in the trunk.

Peg: Is the northern Ohio route <u>quite a bit</u> <u>out of the way</u>?

Pat: Yes. We'll be a lot <u>better off</u> just going down to Flint and then due east through Ontario and across New York on the Thruway.

Peg: And we're still <u>behind the times</u> and don't have an EZ Pass for the New York Thruway.

Pat: Yeah, I know, and we'll have to <u>pay through the nose</u> on the Thruway.

Peg: A 14-hour drive is <u>no picnic</u>. By the time we get there, we'll be ready to <u>call it quits</u>.

40B. Read and fill in the blanks.

Journal entry for January 10

I've been thinking about a change in our marketing plan. Most of our salespeople are <u>on</u> <u>road</u> most of the time, which is <u>no</u> _____ for them. A couple of them are so sick of flying that they're ready to <u>call</u> _____ <u>quits</u>. They routinely spend <u>quite a</u> _____ of psychic energy worrying about getting to client meetings ___ time. Fairly often, one will have to get to a place <u>that's</u> _____ <u>of the way</u>, and they have to take a small feeder airline to get there. The firm <u>pays</u> _____ <u>the nose</u> for those side trips and I think we might be <u>better</u> _____ dropping those clients; in fact, we're just about ___ <u>set</u> to do it. My partner thinks we're <u>behind the</u> _____ because we don't communicate with our clients more via the Net. Perhaps.

80 The Idiom Book

MASSACHUSETTS

40C. Matching Exercise. In the parentheses write the letter of the meaning for each idiom.

Idiom

1) in time ( )
2) on the road ( )
3) all set ( )
4) quite a bit ( )
5) behind the times ( )
6) better off ( )
7) out of the way ( )
8) pay through the nose ( )
9) call it quits ( )
10) no picnic ( )

Meaning

(a) a fairly big amount, degree, or extent
(b) ready; prepared
(c) not too late; early enough
(d) traveling
(e) to pay far too much for something
(f) hard or arduous; unpleasant
(g) to stop working, or stop some activity
(h) not modern; old-fashioned
(i) in a better, or more favorable situation
(j) not in the direct line of travel; hard to get to; remote

40D. Change each of the following sentences with an idiom from 40C.

1) I like to be traveling; going to new places, meeting new people. _____

2) If we hurry we won't be too late. _____

3) I'm ready to start my new job. _____

4) We got a fairly big amount of snow again last night. _____

5) Cooperstown isn't really on our route; do we have to go there? _____

6) We'd be in a better situation if we didn't have to service those clients. _____

7) Uncle Fudd's a little old-fashioned: he still wears galoshes. _____

8) You pay far too much for a sandwich at the airport. _____

9) Driving a truck all day is a hard, demanding job. _____

10) We've done a pretty good day's work. Let's go home. _____

The Idiom Book 81

Lesson 41

NEIGHBORS

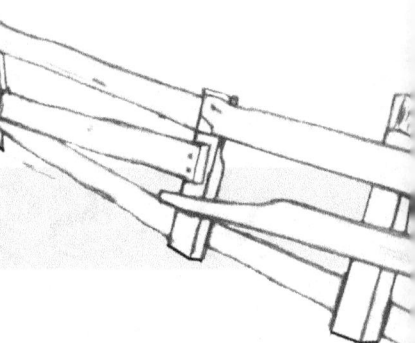

41A. Read.

Linda: We have new neighbors, so let's take over some coffee and <u>start off on the right</u> foot.

Henry: Good idea. <u>You never can tell</u> about people, so let's <u>bend over backwards</u> to try to <u>hit it off</u> with them.

Linda: I think I'll go over with the coffee <u>right now</u> and tell them about trash pickup, holiday service, <u>and so forth</u>.

Henry: And get their names, ages, and occupations <u>while you're at it</u>. And maybe religion, politics, ...

Linda: <u>Heaven forbid</u> that I should ever stoop so low as to become a snoop!

Henry: Just joking, Linda. You know, this isn't a bad neighborhood, <u>all things considered</u>. If these people prove to be civilized, maybe we can stay here <u>after all</u>.

Linda: Henry!

41B. Read and fill in the blanks.

> To: Anne Turpin <AnneT@Officework.com>
> Date: Friday, April 17
> From: Howard <howardP@Officework.com>
> Subject: Stridewell
>
> Anne,
>
>   We may not like it, but Stridewell *is* the new boss, so on Monday let's <u>start off on the right</u> and <u>bend</u> <u>backwards</u> to try to be accommodating. We shouldn't prejudge her; although she was forced on us, she may prove to be a good boss <u>after</u>____.
>   <u>You never</u> <u>tell</u> about people's sensibilities, so I suggest you go in <u>right</u>____ and make sure her office is comfortable, that everything's OK with the desk, computer, intercom, coffee machine and supplies, <u>and so</u>____. And <u>while you're</u> <u>it</u>, get her some kind of welcoming bouquet from the flower shop. Little gestures like that might make it possible for us to <u>hit it</u>____ with her and establish a good working relationship. _____ <u>forbid</u> we have another office massacre! <u>All</u>_____ <u>considered</u>, this is a pretty good place to work; let's try to keep it that way.
>
> P.S. I'll be in at noon after my meeting at Baker's.
>
>   H

41C. Matching Exercise. In the parentheses write the letter of the meaning for each idiom.

Idiom

1) bend over backwards ( )
2) you never can tell ( )
3) start off on the right foot ( )
4) hit it off ( )
5) right now ( )
6) after all ( )
7) heaven forbid ( )
8) while you're at it ( )
9) all things considered ( )
10) and so forth ( )

Meaning

(a) to become friendly
(b) to try very hard
(c) you never know beforehand
(d) make a good beginning
(e) I hope it never happens that . . .
(f) overall
(g) despite everything
(h) at the same time
(i) and similar things
(j) exactly now, not later; immediately

41D. Change each of the following sentences with an idiom from 41C.

1) If we want to make a good beginning, we'll praise him for his wonderful speech. _____

2) You never know beforehand what a new administration will do. _____

3) I've tried very hard to meet her every wish. _____
4) We became friendly with our new neighbors immediately. _____

5) You kids stop that racket immediately, not later. _____

6) I have to get some grommets, wire nuts, connectors, and similar things. _____

7) And please get a new broom at the same time. _____
8) I hope it never happens that I have to work with him again. _____

9) Well, overall, this has been a pretty good year. _____
10) Yeah, we did pretty well although we had a recession. _____

Lesson 42

MANAGEMENT

42A. Read.

Art: So why did you want to see me?

Jake: I'm <u>tickled to death</u>. The answer to our problem was right <u>under my nose</u>.

Art: Well—<u>let's have it</u>.

Jake: I'd been <u>wracking my brain</u> to think who could be our next sales manager, and I just realized that he's already on the staff—Mr. Speaker. He could handle his manager duties <u>as well as</u> his current ones, so we wouldn't have to <u>go to the trouble</u> of replacing him.

Art: <u>I beg to differ</u>. He <u>can no more</u> handle the two jobs <u>than</u> could you or I. There just isn't enough time in the day.

Jake: Then we really are <u>at loggerheads</u> on this, Art. I *know* it'll work.

Art: Jake, I'm afraid we're going to <u>go to the mat</u> on this one.

42B. Read and fill in the blanks.

> To: Jake Reiner <JacobReiner@J&BCO.com>
> Date: Wedneday, June 20
> From: Arthur Blomberg <ArthurBlomberg@J&BCO.com>
> Subject: What's so funny? Speaker?
>
> Jake, my bullheaded partner,
>
>   OK, you rascal, <u>let's</u> _____ it. Something happened <u>right</u> _____ <u>my nose</u> that's <u>tickled you to</u> _____; I don't know what it was, but you're going to tell me. Aren't you? I've been <u>wracking my</u> _____ to think what could make a sourpuss like you so lighthearted, but I'm stumped. I'm your partner, and I'm miffed <u>as</u> _____ <u>as</u> a little hurt that you're being so secretive.
>
>   New subject: I know you think Speaker is right for the manager job, but <u>I beg</u> _____ <u>differ</u>. In my opinion, he <u>can</u> _____ <u>more</u> handle that job <u>than</u> he can run the Pentagon; he's just too immature. I know you've <u>gone to</u> _____ <u>trouble</u> to try to get him ready to do the job, but if you persist, you and I are going to <u>go to</u> _____ <u>mat</u> over this. I probably feel more strongly about it than even you do; I don't want to be <u>at</u> _____ with my partner, so please think about it.
>
>   Jake

DIFFERENCES

42C. Matching Exercise. In the parentheses write the letter of the meaning for each idiom.

Idiom

1) let's have it ( )
2) wrack one's brain ( )
3) under one's nose ( )
4) tickled to death ( )
5) can no more . . . than. . . . ( )
6) as well as ( )
7) beg to differ ( )
8) go to the trouble ( )
9) at loggerheads ( )
10) go to the mat ( )

Meaning

(a) to think very hard
(b) tell me
(c) present and easy to see or understand
(d) quite happy; delighted
(e) can't any more easily [verb phrase] than . . .
(f) seriously quarrelling or arguing
(g) to fight or struggle until one person wins
(h) to firmly disagree with what someone else has said
(i) to use time and effort in (doing something)
(j) and also

42D. Change each of the following sentences with an idiom from 42C.

1) I'm delighted that Minnie got that promotion. _____
2) I looked and looked for my wallet, and it was right on my desk. _____
3) You've got the solution, huh? Tell us what it is. _____
4) For a week I've been trying to determine how to juggle the house closing, the operation, and the hearing all in one day. _____
5) She's kind and gracious, and also extremely funny. _____
6) You know, I spent a lot of time and effort in trying to help you. _____
7) I respectfully disagree with that statement. _____
8) You can't any more easily climb that mountain than you can speak Mongolian. _____
9) They're arguing seriously over who should become sales manager. _____
10) They're going to struggle with this until there's a clear winner. _____

Lesson 43

ESL

43A. Read.

Eve: Helen told me you discovered ESL <u>by accident</u>.

Dot: Yes. In the 1980s, a lot of Ukrainian and Russian refugees settled in our town. I <u>happen to</u> speak some Russian, so I got drafted to teach English as a second language to some of them.

Eve: She says that when working with refugee students, you have to <u>take into account</u> a lot more than linguistic issues: things like health, money, work, family size, history, religion.

Dot: Uh huh. Being a refugee in a strange land and culture, where even the writing system is exotic, and being broke <u>in the bargain</u>, is <u>a dog's life</u>. You *do* have to appreciate that.

Eve: She says that most of them <u>take advantage of</u> whatever help the town and state offer and <u>make do</u>.

Dot: Yes, of course. They have to, because <u>no matter</u> what happens to them in the States, they're refugees and can't go back. And plenty happens. Their kids are almost always desperately homesick for their old friends, and pets, and neighborhood, and are hit hard by <u>culture shock</u>—in school, in the neighborhood, everywhere. It didn't take me long to start to <u>get a feel for</u> some of what these people face every day. I soon realized that the ESL instructor here is very often the refugee's only window on North American culture. That realization can be daunting.

43B. Read and fill in the blanks.

Journal Entry for September 1

Interesting, isn't it, the paths our lives take. It was quite <u>by</u> _____ that I became a part-time auto electrician. I _____ <u>to be</u> aware of Ohm's Law, and when my friends learned that I could distinguish between a faulty alternator and a worn-out battery, I became really popular. You have to <u>take</u> _____ <u>account</u> that most of us then were <u>making</u> __ on very little money, really living <u>a dog's</u> _____ financially and driving old clunkers <u>in</u> <u>the</u> _____. My friends didn't _____ <u>advantage of</u> me; they just asked for help because they needed it; we were all poor. And ____ <u>matter</u> the reason, if I needed a small loan then, I could always get it from one of them. When I think of the old friends that I can still see, at least occasionally, I ____ <u>a feel for</u> what my refugee students have lost because they can't see their old friends any more. Now that's real <u>culture</u> _____, that kind of new and painful hole in one's life caused by a forced move to a new and different society.

43C. Matching Exercise. In the parentheses write the letter of the meaning for each idiom.

Idiom

1) happen to ( )
2) by accident ( )
3) take into account ( )
4) in the bargain ( )
5) make do ( )
6) get a feel for ( )
7) a dog's life ( )
8) no matter ( )
9) culture shock ( )
10) take advantage of ( )

Meaning

(a) also
(b) to realize, consider, or be aware of; remember
(c) incidentally or fortuitously be or do something
(d) accidentally; not as something planned
(e) regardless of
(f) confusion and discomfort from being in a new and strange life
(g) to begin to understand something
(h) cope, or manage
(i) to use, or utilize, something or someone, sometimes unfairly
(j) a wretched, miserable life for a human

43D. Change each of the following sentences with an idiom from 43C.

1) But officer, I hit her with my car through no fault of my own. _____

2) Incidentally, I'm rich and powerful. _____
3) You have to realize that he's just a kid and doesn't understand what's happening. _____

4) She left him and also took all his money. _____
5) He has led a miserable existence since she left him. _____

6) You should use this opportunity while you have time. _____

7) They're coping, with almost no help from their parents. _____

8) Regardless of what happens, you will always be welcome here. _____

9) The kids are experiencing confusion, discomfort, and unhappiness living in a new country. _____

10) I'm starting to understand how to use my new computer. _____

Lesson 44

 EXERCISE

44A. Read.

Jorge: Hello, how can I help you?

Lupita: I'm here because I need to get <u>in shape</u>.

Jorge: You know, that requires exercising four or five times a week.

Lupita: I want to do it the right way, right from <u>square one</u>!

Jorge: That's <u>the ticket</u>! Discipline and the right attitude.

Lupita: I want to get <u>off to a good start</u>.

Jorge: Now let's be clear about this: <u>a good number of</u> hopefuls have begun this program, but <u>a number of</u> candidates have quit in midstream, <u>brought up short</u> by the fact that the regimen's <u>anything but</u> easy and <u>nothing but</u> vigorous physical exertion.

Lupita: Let's begin now, <u>in earnest</u>.

44B. Read and fill in the blanks.

```
                          MEMO
              State University Athletics Department
To: Asst. coaches                           Date: September 5
From: Coach Vigger                          Re: Discipline
```

To get this team __*shape*__, we're going to have to go back to _____ *one*: training discipline. I think that's _____ *ticket* for getting them *off to a* _____ *start*. __*A good*_____ of teams have failed because of poor training habits, and *a number* _____ coaches have been fired for the same reason. Not me. It <u>brought the director</u> _____ <u>short</u> when I asked him for more time for practice; he said he thought I should get less time with the kids. I told him that our job was to produce athletes, not scholars; that the job was *anything* _____ simple; and that we were interested in _____ *but* victory for the team. That's when the discussion began _____ *earnest*. In the end, he said, "I want to see a winner."

88 The Idiom Book

44C. Matching Exercise. In the parentheses write the letter of the meaning for each idiom.

Idiom

1) square one ( )
2) in shape ( )
3) off to a good start ( )
4) the ticket ( )
5) in earnest ( )
6) bring up short ( )
7) a number of ( )
8) anything but ( )
9) nothing but ( )
10) a good number of ( )

Meaning

(a) beginning well
(b) exactly right
(c) the very beginning
(d) physically fit
(e) definitely not
(f) always and only
(g) seriously and truly
(h) to surprise and confuse someone and make that person stop suddenly
(i) some; an unspecified number
(j) a lot; many

44D. Change each of the following sentences with an idiom from 44C.

1) Mr. Chubb, you're just not physically fit. I think you should start dieting and exercising.

2) We'll have to go back to the very beginning to determine what happened. _____

3) That's exactly right: long walks and a diet heavy on fruit and veggies. _____

4) The team's made a good beginning: three wins and no losses. _____

5) A lot of us are getting together for a party before the big game. _____

6) There's more than one time that I regretted saying that. _____

7) The remark surprised and confused her, and she stopped talking. _____

8) She's certainly not ill-mannered. _____

9) He's always courteous. _____

10) The Middle East participants began discussing the issues seriously this morning. _____

Lesson 45

POLITICS

45A. Read.

Richard: When there's an election in this country, you never really know why somebody has <u>thrown their hat in the ring</u>.

Ronald: I disagree. It seems to me fairly obvious sometimes that some <u>run for office</u> to be <u>of service</u> to the people, and some do it <u>in order to</u> be able to loot the public treasury.

Richard: Well, I think you will agree that <u>politics makes strange bedfellows</u>, literally. Fairly often, members of the same household have nothing <u>in common</u> but their politics. <u>Then again</u>, in some families, spouses' votes will sometimes neutralize each other.

Ronald: The neighbors on either side of me <u>hold in high esteem</u> a national politician whom I consider <u>beneath contempt</u>, and I <u>think a lot of</u> those neighbors. They're really nice folks.

45B. Read and fill in the blanks.

Journal Entry for January 15

After a week or so as co-chair for the People's Progressive Party, I think I'm enjoying it.

You know, it is true that <u>politics</u> _____ <u>strange bedfellows</u>: I'm in the same political party as Herbert Wilson, who's _____ <u>contempt</u> in his business practices. I don't like him, but ____ <u>again</u> he votes right, so he and I are co-chairs of the county committee. What we <u>have</u> _____ <u>common</u> is the aims of the party. Period.

When you <u>throw your</u> _____ <u>in the ring</u> for any state or national office, you usually recite the usual reason: "I'm <u>running</u> _____ <u>office</u> <u>in</u> _____ <u>to</u> be _____ <u>service</u> to the people," etc. Surprisingly, and despite the cynicism that is almost always expressed when politics is discussed, I'm happy to say that there are quite a few politicians that I <u>think a</u> _____ <u>of</u>, and a few that I actually <u>hold in</u> _____ <u>esteem</u>. Let's hope we can re-elect them.

45C. Matching Exercise. In the parentheses write the letter of the meaning for each idiom.

Idiom

1) throw one's hat in the ring (   )
2) in order to (   )
3) of service (   )
4) run for office (   )
5) think a lot of someone (   )
6) have something in common (   )
7) then again (   )
8) hold in high esteem (   )
9) politics makes strange bedfellows (   )
10) beneath contempt (   )

Meaning

(a) for this purpose:
(b) helpful
(c) to try to win an election
(d) to announce that you are going to try to win an election
(e) to admire (someone) greatly
(f) despicable and worthless
(g) to like someone
(h) however
(i) to be similar in some way
(j) politics can make very different people cooperate for some purpose

45D. Change each of the following sentences with an idiom from 45C.

1) She had a meeting to announce that she intends to run for city council. _____

2) She's trying to win a seat on the city council. _____
3) If I win the election, I honestly intend to be helpful to my constituents. _____

4) We undercoated the car so as to make it more resistant to rust. _____

5) A political campaign can produce some incongruous alliances. _____

6) They have similar outlooks in the way they view the war. _____

7) I love the ice and snow of winter. However, I'm not too fond of the heating bills. _____

8) We really admire that politician. She's actually honest. _____

9) That liar and thief is really worthless. _____
10) I'm lucky: I like my neighbors a lot. _____

The Idiom Book 91

Lesson 46

DOWNSIZED

46A. Read.

Matt: Hi, Kate. How was your day?

Kate: <u>I've had it</u>! We're being downsized and I <u>got the boot</u>.

Matt: Man—we'll be <u>up the creek</u> if one of us doesn't get something else right away.

Kate: I wonder about this economic recovery that the president says is <u>just around the corner</u>.

Matt: Sure it is. I might <u>try my hand</u> at the dynamite factory. My brother *is* a <u>big wheel</u> over there.

Kate: And if somebody makes a bad mistake, you might get <u>blown to smithereens</u>.

Matt: Well, we have to do *something*. And the <u>pickings</u> around here are pretty <u>slim</u>.

Kate: Granted. But don't <u>go off half-cocked</u> and risk your life over there. It's not as if the economy is <u>in a shambles</u>. I'll find work.

46B. Read and fill in the blanks.

A Note from the Desk of Vance Robinson

Saturday, May 3

Dear Lil,

Your son and his wife left the rec room <u>in a</u> _____ , and <u>I've</u> ____ <u>it</u> with them. I'm going to evict them. They never pay the rent on time, anyway, and I'm not really surprised that Josh <u>got</u> ____ boot at the Institute. He's irresponsible as a tenant and was obviously the same way as an employee. The _____ <u>are slim</u> around here for job-hunters, so he'll be ____ <u>the creek</u> looking for work with a lousy recommendation. It seems to me that he should <u>try</u> ____ hand at something he's suited for: an entry-level job that he could learn to perform well after a few years. But he's already a ____ <u>wheel</u> in his own mind, so he'll probably <u>go</u> ____ <u>half-cocked</u> again and grab something flashy that he can't handle, and get fired again. I'd say that bankruptcy's ____ <u>around the corner</u> for them. Poor you. Once more, he's <u>blown</u> your hopes and plans ____ <u>smithereens</u>.

Cousin Vance

92 The Idiom Book

46C. Matching Exercise. In the parentheses write the letter of the meaning for each idiom.

Idiom

1) just around the corner (   )
2) get the boot (   )
3) up the creek (   )
4) have had it (   )
5) go off half-cocked (   )
6) big wheel (   )
7) blow to smithereens (   )
8) slim pickings (   )
9) try one's hand (   )
10) in a shambles (   )

Meaning

(a) coming soon; imminent
(b) in a very bad, unpleasant situation
(c) to be fired from a job
(d) to be frustrated, and angry
(e) very few chances or opportunities
(f) to do something too soon and without thinking carefully
(g) a situation or place that is in complete disorder
(h) to explode and break into very small pieces
(i) an important person
(j) to try to do something for the first time

46D. Change each of the following sentences with an idiom from 46C.

1) Now we're in real trouble. I just lost my job. [Two idioms] _____

2) They're in a terrible fix: they got evicted from their house. _____

3) The president tells us every week the economic recovery will be very soon. _____

4) I've never done any snowboarding. I think I'll try it. _____

5) Cousin Clyde is a boss down at the bakery. _____

6) A gas leak demolished the house. _____

7) There sure aren't many jobs around here. _____

8) Don't agree to this offer too fast. Give it some very careful thought. _____

9) After the kids' game down there, the basement was a mess—disorderly and dirty. _____

The Idiom Book

Lesson 47
BASHFUL BOY

47A. Read.

Rod: I saw Maria today.

Ted: Have you managed to <u>make contact</u> with her yet? Like, actually talked to her?

Rod: No. She's never <u>by herself</u>.

Ted: Look. Pick up the phone and <u>give her a buzz</u>. You<u>'ve got nothing to lose</u>.

[Later]

Ted: Well, did you <u>get up your courage</u> and call her?

Rod: Yes I did. She sounds really nice.

Ted: <u>It's about time</u>. What's your next move? You're not going to <u>sweep her off her feet</u> by standing around daydreaming about her.

Rod: You know, you're <u>long on</u> advice when it's somebody else who's <u>sticking his neck out</u>. I think I can struggle along without your guidance <u>from now on</u>.

Ted: Hey! I'm only trying to help.

47B. Read and fill in the blanks.

> rrrrring
>
> This is H. G. Smithson. I'm not in. Please leave a message.
>
>   Harry, this is your brother. I got your call, but listen, you have to start acting instead of just reacting. You can't _____ <u>contact</u> with the director by sitting around ___<u>yourself</u> and telling yourself that you just don't have any luck. You've got to <u>get</u> _____ <u>your courage</u>—you<u>'ve got nothing</u> _____ <u>lose</u>. Just _____ <u>her a buzz</u>. Get on the phone and do it! If you can't reach her, use that fabled charm of yours and try to <u>sweep her receptionist</u> _____ <u>her feet</u> and get at least a telephone interview with the director. I <u>stuck my neck</u> ____ for you when I should have, little brother, and <u>it's about</u> _____ for you to act. _____ <u>now on</u>, you have to act like a grownup. You're <u>long</u> ____ grand plans for the future, now make them happen. And don't call me back!

94   The Idiom Book

47C. Matching Exercise. In the parentheses write the letter of the meaning for each idiom.

Idiom

1) by herself ( )
2) make contact ( )
3) nothing to lose ( )
4) give someone a buzz ( )
5) long on ( )
6) stick one's neck out ( )
7) sweep her off her feet ( )
8) get up one's courage ( )
9) it's about time ( )
10) from now on ( )

Meaning

(a) to call (someone) by telephone
(b) no need to be afraid
(c) alone
(d) to establish communication
(e) having, or supplied with, plenty of something
(f) to take a risk
(g) continuing forever, from this time
(h) to overwhelm (someone) emotionally
(i) finally
(j) to force oneself to be brave

47D. Change each of the following sentences with an idiom from 47C.

1) The first thing we have to do is establish communication with our representative. _____

2) She's standing there by the sea, all alone. _____

3) Use the phone and see if you can reach them. _____

4) Go ahead. She might say no, but so what? _____

5) Be brave! Ask her for a dance. _____

6) It's late, but you did get here. Finally. _____

7) I used my charm to overwhelm her emotionally and romantically. _____

8) He has plenty of advice on how other people should live. _____

9) I'm going to take a risk and say what I really think. _____

10) From this time forward, you are NOT to come home later than 10 o'clock at night! _____

The Idiom Book 95

Lesson 48

BASIC TRAINING

48A. Read.

Jeff, Jr.: Dad, when you were in the army, what was basic training like?

Jeff, Sr.: When I was in basic training, there was a guy in my squad who had five kids. And <u>to make matters worse</u>, he'd already <u>done his bit</u> in a previous war. I thought the draft board must have <u>had it in for</u> him, but he didn't <u>hold it against</u> the board; he said he figured they just weren't too <u>swift on the uptake</u>.

Jeff, Jr.: I've heard basic training <u>has a way of</u> puncturing inflated egos.

Jeff, Sr.: Yes. All the recruits are <u>treated like dirt</u>. Misery loves company; a lot of the recruits are still <u>wet behind the ears</u>, so they cling together and form pretty close bonds, which is good for them and for the squad.

Jeff, Jr.: I guess they find themselves <u>up against</u> people, things, and situations that are new and scary.

Jeff, Sr.: Right, and that's when the instructors try to teach them to <u>keep their heads</u> and depend on each other. It helps to have a buddy in a situation like that.

48B. Read and fill in the blanks.

Dear Diary,

Although Junior is still <u>wet behind the   </u>, and the machine operators are <u>treating him like   </u>, he's <u>keeping   </u> head. He's <u>   against</u> a lot of antagonism; the operators <u>have it in   </u> him because he's the boss's son, and they <u>   it against</u> him, as if he's wronged them. But despite the poisonous atmosphere, he <u>does his   </u> when there's a need for a twelve-hour shift because of a rush order. And <u>to   </u> matters worse, in a sense, he *is* <u>swift   </u> the uptake with his understanding of the machinery, and he does <u>have a   of</u> charming the lady operators. It'll be a while before he wins any popularity contests among the men.

48C. Matching Exercise. In the parentheses write the letter of the meaning for each idiom.

Idiom

1) to make matters worse ( )
2) have it in for ( )
3) do one's bit ( )
4) hold something against someone ( )
5) up against ( )
6) treat like dirt ( )
7) have a way of ( )
8) wet behind the ears ( )
9) swift on the uptake ( )
10) keep one's head ( )

Meaning

(a) to dislike someone because of a past action
(b) to intend to hurt someone because of a grudge
(c) to perform one's part, or duty, in a group effort
(d) what is even worse is that . . .
(e) to stay calm and not panic
(f) facing, or contending with
(g) not grown up
(h) to behave harshly and contemptuously toward someone
(i) to usually be efficient or competent at (doing something)
(j) fast to learn; intelligent

48D. Change each of the following sentences with an idiom from 48C.

1) Clyde doesn't brush his teeth very often; and what's worse is that he loves to chew garlic. _____

2) She always does her share of the work. _____

3) The coach has a grudge against me. I'll never get to play. _____

4) I fumbled on the last play of the game last week, and I know he dislikes me because of that. _____

5) Annie's a fast learner: she mastered quadratic equations in one lesson. _____

6) She's pretty good at getting what she wants from her teachers. _____

7) The kids who cook in that fast-food joint have horrible working conditions. _____

8) The ones in the cleaning crew look as if they're still teenagers. _____

9) When we play these guys next week, we'll be competing with the state champs. _____

10) If you guys don't panic, we can beat them. _____

The Idiom Book

Lesson 49
ROCK CLIMBING

49A. Read.

Mark: Amanda, it's a glorious day. We have ropes and carabiners, so let's <u>put them to use</u>.

Amanda: We could <u>make a day of it</u> at Chapel Ledge.

Mark: OK. If you pack some apples and oranges, I'll stow the gear and we can be <u>on our way</u>.

[At the climbing site]

Mark: Now, Mandy—if you're going to belay me, I don't want any <u>funny business</u>.

Amanda: <u>Perish the thought</u>! You know, you're not such a bad climber, for a man, <u>that is</u>.

Mark: Don't be a <u>smart ass</u>. Get that rope to me, will you?

Amanda: <u>Bear with me</u>. Fran was telling me a couple of days ago that she and her husband think that anybody who climbs is <u>asking for it</u>.

Mark: I think they talk that way because they just don't have <u>what it takes</u>.

49B. Read and fill in the blanks.

From: John A. Carlson jackAC@Topnet.com
Date: March 25
To: Jill Peterson <JillP@southway.net>
Subject: A Trip to DC

Hi Jill,

    I may have thought of a way to <u>put</u>   <u>use</u> my skill as a smooth talker: I've applied for a position as a press secretary for a politician. We could visit the capital, and you could <u>make</u>   <u>day of it</u> at the tourist attractions there while I try to persuade Representative O'Connor that I've got <u>what</u>   <u>takes</u> to handle his problems; <u>that</u> , the <u>funny</u>   he's allegedly been doing. I certainly don't mean that I would lie for him—<u>perish</u>   <u>thought</u>. I do mean that I can probably handle those big-city reporters; they're a bunch of _____ <u>asses</u> who're just _____ <u>for it</u>, and I'm the guy who can deliver. <u>On</u>   <u>way</u> to the capital, we can plan your sightseeing. And please <u>bear</u>   <u>me</u>—I'll find work.

Jack

98 The Idiom Book

48C. Matching Exercise. In the parentheses write the letter of the meaning for each idiom.

Idiom

1) on one's way ( )
2) make a day of it ( )
3) put something to use ( )
4) funny business ( )
5) ask for it ( )
6) that is [that IZ] ( )
7) smart ass ( )
8) bear with me ( )
9) perish the thought ( )
10) what it takes ( )

Meaning

(a) trickery or dishonesty
(b) (while) going or traveling somewhere
(c) to spend a day in some pleasant activity
(d) to utilize, or use, something
(e) don't be cross or impatient
(f) to deliberately be doing something that will probably cause trouble
(g) an essential element, component, or trait
(h) someone impudent, disrespectful, funny, and also irritating
(i) [1] is what I mean to say; [2] what I mean is. . . .
(j) don't even think that

49D. Change each of the following sentences with an idiom from 49C.

1) You paid 200 bucks for that gadget in the garage, and you've never used it. _____

2) Let's spend the whole day at the science museum. It's a wonderful place. _____

3) Let's stop for breakfast before we get to Frankfurt. _____

4) He's being investigated for some kind of dishonesty to do with gamblers. _____

5) Our representative take a bribe? Don't even think it! _____

6) He's absolutely honest. What I mean is, he's never been caught. _____

7) That kid is disrespectful and disagreeable. _____
8) I'm going as fast as I can. Please be patient. _____
9) When you tease that dog like that, you're inviting it to bite you. _____

10) I think I have the essential traits of a good spokesman. _____

The Idiom Book   99

Lesson 50
BASKETBALL WIN

50A. Read.

Abdul: We beat them 54 to 30. <u>Cleaned their clock</u>.

Melody: You really <u>kicked ass</u>. <u>No wonder</u> you look so pleased.

Abdul: Yeah. We're finally <u>getting our act together</u>.

Melody: I thought they'd <u>make mincemeat of</u> you. I guess maybe they've been <u>top dog</u> for so long that they got overconfident.

Abdul: Maybe, but <u>for once</u>, everything worked right for us. We were <u>in no mood to</u> lose today, and we <u>went to town on</u> them right from the tip-off.

Melody: That game was <u>one for the books</u>.

50B. Read and fill in the blanks.

From: Basil Roberts <basilsplace@Supersend.com>
Date: October 15
To: Clint West <clintwest_MorrillHall@OSU.edu>
Subject: Disaster@TUHS

Clint,

   I'm glad you made the team at State U. We sure miss you here. It's been a terrible season so far. The Springfield Rangers <u>cleaned</u> clock good; they <u>kicked</u> and <u>made mincemeat</u> us. <u>wonder</u> all the papers rate them <u>top</u>. Now, I hope we can <u>get</u> act together and <u>go</u> town on Hartford High <u>for</u>, but I don't know if we'll ever manage that either.

   Well, I'm <u>in</u> mood to tell you anymore just how bad we are this year, except to admit to you privately that our performance has been so pathetic that this season is going to be <u>one</u> the books.

Basil

50C. Matching Exercise. In the parentheses write the letter of the meaning for each idiom.

Idiom

1) clean one's clock ( )
2) kick ass [coarse and informal] ( )
3) no wonder ( )
4) get one's act together ( )
5) make mincemeat of ( )
6) top dog ( )
7) for once ( )
8) in no mood ( )
9) go to town on ( )
10) one for the books ( )

Meaning

(a) to start acting effectively and efficiently
(b) it isn't surprising that. . . .
(c) to win decisively
(d) to defeat badly
(e) determined not (to do something)
(f) to treat someone or something in a vigorous, energetic way
(g) something outstanding or unique
(h) at last; finally
(i) the best, strongest, or most powerful one in a group
(j) to defeat decisively

50D. Change each of the following sentences with an idiom from 50C.

1) Man, the Rounders really whipped the Bounders. _____

2) The Rounders won overwhelmingly. _____

3) It's not surprising you're gaining weight: you never exercise. _____

4) Henry's starting to become a lot more efficient. _____

5) The Bounders just thrashed the Rounders. _____

6) Tom Goode is the best competitor in the whole meet. _____

7) Well—you finally got to work on time. _____

8) I'm certainly not going to listen to your complaints right now. _____

9) He worked hard on that firewood this morning. It's all split and stacked. _____

10) Her performance at the concert was outstanding. _____

Lesson 51
AT THE COTTAGE

51A. Read.

Gale: There's a storm <u>on the way</u>—we'd better get ready for it.

Ralph: OK. I'll secure the boat, <u>just in case</u>.

Gale: Look at those thunderheads. We'd better <u>make tracks</u> for the cottage.

Ralph: Yeah—let's <u>hightail it</u>.

Gale: I hope we've got candles and matches. The power company can't <u>hack it</u> here during a storm.

Ralph: We're OK. We'll be <u>as snug as a bug in a rug</u>.

Gale: Do you think we'll get back here <u>before snow flies</u>?

Ralph: Oh sure. We've got all of October <u>to go</u> yet. And <u>in any event</u>, we have to get back here before winter, because we have to get the place ready for winter before we <u>wrap things up</u> for the year.

51B. Read and fill in the blanks.

From: Carl Howard <carlhoward@speedwell_inc>
Date: February 24
To: Rose Howard <rosehoward@FamilyInstitute.org>

Rose,

There's real trouble <u>on</u> _____ <u>way</u> for the firm because the directors just can't <u>hack</u> _____ in today's world of globalization, downsizing, etc. I've sent out 15 resumes <u>just in</u> _____, and I think I'll probably get a few responses. _____ <u>any event</u>, responses or not, things have got so poisonous here that I'm going to <u>hightail</u> _____ out of here as soon as I can. I've arranged my work in such a way that, if I get a decent job offer, I could _____ <u>things up</u> here in one day and _____ <u>tracks</u> back to you and take maybe a week at home before I started the new job.

You know, just a few years ago, we were <u>as snug as a</u> _____ <u>in a rug</u> in our home, a nice "secure" job, etc., and now.... A big concern in August used to be ,"We've got to close the cottage <u>before snow</u> _____." Now my concern is starting to be "I've still got 15 years <u>go</u> before I can retire. But will I be able to retire?"

Carl

102   The Idiom Book

51C. Matching Exercise. In the parentheses write the letter of the meaning for each idiom.

Idiom

1) on the way ( )
2) hightail it ( )
3) just in case ( )
4) make tracks ( )
5) wrap things up ( )
6) hack it ( )
7) snug as a bug in a rug ( )
8) before snow flies ( )
9) to go ( )
10) in any event ( )

Meaning

(a) to leave, or go away, fast
(b) as a precaution
(c) to run away from something fast
(d) approaching
(e) before winter begins
(f) still remaining [of time or distance]
(g) warm, safe, and comfortable; cozy
(h) regardless of anything else
(i) to work, or act, efficiently or competently
(j) to end a process, job, or activity

51D. Change each of the following sentences with an idiom from 51C.

1) Look at the western sky. There's a storm coming. _____

2) I brought my umbrella as a precaution. I don't like the way the sky looks. _____

3) Hey, look at that lightning! Let's run for the house! _____

4) There's the bell. I have to leave right away. _____

5) That so-called computer technician is just incompetent: my computer's always crashing. _____

6) The kids are all warm and cozy in their beds. _____

7) We've got to fix that heater before winter begins. _____

8) We still have 200 miles to travel before we get to Calgary. _____

9) I'm leaving this job, whatever happens. _____

10) Let's finish what we're doing here and go home. _____

The Idiom Book

Lesson 52
NATIONAL LEADERS

52A. Read.

Peter: The leader of our nation spoke on TV last night. What I heard was <u>hot air</u>.

Ellen: Yes—I heard about how all our efforts abroad are <u>coming up roses</u>. These great leaders either won't or can't deliver <u>the straight goods</u> when they talk to their people. I guess it <u>goes with the territory</u>.

Peter: Well, they look at, and explain, <u>what's going on</u> according to their own <u>frame of reference</u> and from their own <u>point of view</u>.

Ellen: Which means that plain truth <u>goes out the window</u>.

Peter: That, unfortunately, <u>goes without saying</u>.

Ellen: Well, I might do the same <u>in their shoes</u>.

52B. Read and fill in the blanks.

From: Bertha G. Washington <BGW.WashingtonGroup@Pittsteelco.com>
Date: December 12
To: Charles Washington <charles@Idaho_mining.com>
Subject: Aluminum

Charlie,

It's nice to hear that everything's <u>coming</u> _____ <u>roses</u> in your bauxite venture. I hope you're giving me <u>the</u> _____ <u>goods</u> and not just a lot of _____ <u>air</u>! I appreciate that a tendency to embroider the truth <u>goes</u> _____ <u>the territory</u> in sales work, but I'm sure that you'd never try to deceive your own mother.

Incidentally, if I were <u>in</u> _____ <u>shoes</u>, I'd pay a lot of attention to _____ <u>going on</u> in China. They're buying, among other things, a lot of aluminum as part of the industrial expansion, so maybe you should consider going over there before this opportunity for a nice contract <u>goes</u> _____ <u>the window</u>. And it <u>goes</u> _____ <u>saying</u> that if you do go, you should be careful. (Consider my _____ <u>of view</u> as your mother.) And of course I know you'll remember that the Chinese have a <u>frame of</u> _____ that's a bit different from yours.

Love,
Mom

104 The Idiom Book

52C. Matching Exercise. In the parentheses write the letter of the meaning for each idiom.

Idiom

1) hot air ( )
2) goes with the territory ( )
3) the straight goods ( )
4) coming up roses ( )
5) point of view ( )
6) frame of reference ( )
7) what's going on ( )
8) goes without saying ( )
9) goes out the window ( )
10) in someone's shoes ( )

Meaning

(a) is an inevitable, or unavoidable, aspect of something
(b) honesty; the truth
(c) developing, or ending, well
(d) meaningless talk; nonsense
(e) disappears, or vanishes
(f) is clearly true
(g) experiencing what someone else is experiencing
(h) one's way of understanding or judging something
(i) the culture, knowledge, and experience that influence how you think
(j) interesting, important activities in progress

52D. Change each of the following sentences with an idiom from 52C.

1) Congresswoman Bloward delivered one of her typical speeches. It was empty nonsense. ___

2) Everything's developing quite nicely in her new business. ___

3) My mechanic always gives me the truth. It's a pleasure to do business with him. ___

4) Making difficult decisions is part of a commander's job. ___

5) He's quite unaware of the important changes happening in this country right now. ___

6) Her sensibilities were formed partly by events of 60 years ago. ___

7) From my way of seeing things, these recent court decisions make for bad public policy. ___

8) When that extremist entered the negotiations, any possibility of compromise vanished. ___

9) It should be obvious that you're welcome to stay here. ___

10) If I were you, I'd be looking for a different job. ___

Lesson 53

TALK SHOW

 **53A. Read.**

Harry: Here at the *Harry at Ten* talk show we'd like to welcome once again Dr. Sterling Pound. Dr. Pound, welcome to the show. We're anxious to hear about your new book, *The New Europeans*.

Sterling: Thanks for inviting me, Harry. Let me get right to the point: The EU is <u>here to stay</u>. It includes almost every important country in Europe.

Harry: And in your book, you said their combined power will <u>make for</u> some interesting competition for the Indians, the Japanese, the Americans, and the Chinese.

Sterling: That's <u>putting it mildly</u>.

Harry: Although it will take <u>some doing</u> to compete successfully <u>on the same stage</u> with those giants.

Sterling: I know, but I think that within <u>a matter of</u> ten years <u>or thereabouts</u> the Europeans won't be <u>taking a back seat</u> to anybody in any sphere, even pop culture. They have brains and talent <u>to spare</u>; they'll <u>make a go of</u> it.

53B. Read and fill in the blanks.

Senator Donald E. Golden   May 23
Senate Office Building, Suite 237
Washington, D.C., 20090

Dear Senator Golden:

   I've just come back from the Far East, and I want to let you know what I saw and heard. The energy crisis won't disappear if the price of petroleum dips temporarily to fifty dollars, or twenty dollars, a barrel; it's <u>here to _____</u>. And our drilling for oil in a wildlife refuge instead of trying seriously to develop other energy sources _____ <u>for</u> our *not* being taken seriously by the rest of the world. And that's <u>putting it _____</u>. It will take <u>some _____</u> to get this country to address our energy problem honestly; in fact it will take a different administration. Within <u>matter of</u> five years <u>thereabouts</u>, we'll be competing <u>on the same _____</u> with China for petroleum, because we're just using too much oil, too fast, including our own. China means to <u>make a _____</u> of its immense industrial expansion; it needs huge amounts of foreign oil to fuel the generating stations to power this expansion; and it won't <u>take a _____ seat</u> to anybody in getting access to the oil. It has people and brains <u>_____ spare</u> for this coming struggle; can we say the same?

                                                            Regards,
                                                            Victor Voter, III

106   The Idiom Book

53C. Matching Exercise. In the parentheses write the letter of the meaning for each idiom.

Idiom

1) some doing ( )
2) make for ( )
3) putting it mildly ( )
4) here to stay ( )
5) take a back seat to ( )
6) a matter of ( )
7) or thereabouts ( )
8) on the same stage ( )
9) make a go of ( )
10) to spare ( )

Meaning

(a) a lot of hard work
(b) an understatement
(c) to permit or cause an abstract condition
(d) in existence, and permanent
(e) to be inferior to someone or something else
(f) in abundance
(g) to succeed at something
(h) approximately
(i) an extent [in time, distance, or amount]
(j) on equal terms; equally

53D. Change each of the following sentences with an idiom from 53C.

1) It looks as if global warming might be permanent. _____

2) Her account of conflict with the president and his advisors is material for an interesting article. _____

3) Winter can be a fairly serious matter in northern Alberta, and that's an understatement. ___

4) It will take a lot of work to make this house fit to live in. _____

5) We'll be competing on equal terms with Germans and Japanese for buyers. _____

6) They hauled the boats overland from the falls to the fort, a distance of three miles. _____

7) She was a handsome woman of 60, approximately. _____

8) Women always have to accept inferior status in that society. _____

9) We've got plenty of extra time, so let's grab lunch. _____

10) Do you think they'll succeed in the business? _____

Lesson 54

TRAVELING

54A. Read.

Victor: Well, George, <u>I'm about to</u> leave for Chengdu with stops in Tel Aviv and Amman.

George: If you're <u>headed for</u> central China, why <u>in the world</u> are you going <u>by way of</u> the Middle East?

Victor: As you know, things <u>at present</u> are <u>in flux</u> in Amman and Tel Aviv; if you want to know what's happening in places like that, you have to be there <u>on the ground</u>. And besides that, I have to <u>mend fences</u> in both places because our reps there <u>stepped on some toes</u> last week. I didn't realize I'd have to <u>keep tabs on</u> those two.

George: I think you should fire them.

Victor: We'll see.

54B. Read and fill in the blanks.

From: Hyacinth Porter <hyper3@Silvernet.com>
Date: June 7
To: Richard Porter <RPorter@Porter_Cabot_and Lodge.com>
Subject: Bunny!!!!

Richard,

    I tried calling you at the office, but you weren't there. I think you should know about this so I'm emailing.

    I'm all packed for Manchester and I <u>was</u> just <u>about</u> walk out the door when Bunny called and told me that she was <u>headed</u> her mother's place in London. When I asked what <u>the world</u> was happening, she said that she was going to live with her mother, and was going to go <u>by way</u> Worcester and stop at her lawyer's office and start divorce proceedings against Claude. So things are <u>present</u> rather <u>flux</u> here; you really have to be here <u>the ground</u> to appreciate just how much in flux. I apparently <u>stepped</u> <u>some toes</u> last week when I offered helpful advice on marriage to Bunny and Claude. Instead of being grateful, they flew into a rage. That's the kind of thanks you get when you try to help people. Now it seems I should have tried to <u>mend</u>   . Those two need someone to <u>tabs on</u> them and keep them from assassinating each other.

                                        Gotta run,
                                        Cynth

54C. Matching Exercise. In the parentheses write the letter of the meaning for each idiom.

Idiom

1) be about to (   )
2) headed for (   )
3) by way of (   )
4) in the world (   )
5) mend fences (   )
6) keep tabs on (   )
7) on the ground (   )
8) at present (   )
9) step on toes (   )
10) in flux (   )

Meaning

(a) via
(b) [used for emphasis.]
(c) going or traveling to . . .
(d) almost ready to do something
(e) to improve poor social or diplomatic relations
(f) to offend someone by interfering in their business or affairs
(g) to watch and control the behavior of a person or group
(h) in the real place where something important is happening
(i) to be changing a lot
(j) currently; now

54D. Change each of the following sentences with an idiom from 54C.

1) We were just getting ready to eat when the doorbell rang. _____

2) So long. I'm on my way to Vladivostok. _____
3) This doesn't make sense. Why would you try to impress her?! _____

4) We drove to Regina via some back roads. _____
5) Currently, I'm awaiting a new assignment. _____
6) The situation at headquarters is changing. _____
7) If you want to know what's happening in the war, you have to be where the war is. _____

8) I have to apologize for some things I said at the wedding reception. _____

9) She offended Tom when she told him how to handle the dissension in his unit. _____

10) Her kids are wild and undisciplined. She doesn't always know where they are. _____

The Idiom Book   109

Lesson 55
FLYING FIRST CLASS

55A. Read.

Jose: Victor! How nice to see you. Are you on this flight to London?
Victor: I am, Jose. But on to Tel Aviv, Amman, and Chengdu, first class, thankfully.
Jose: Hmm. If you're flying first class, you must be a <u>big cheese</u> at Electronics, Inc.
Victor: Yeah, I'm living <u>high off the hog</u>.
Jose: I suppose they <u>stuck it to</u> you for the ticket.
Victor: I don't know—the company <u>foots the bill</u> and I didn't ask. And they've arranged for a car and driver to be <u>at my disposal</u> all the time that I'm in Chengdu.
Jose: Huh. They <u>have a good opinion of</u> you. Have you possibly <u>changed your mind</u> about leaving the firm?
Victor: Yes, I have. I've discovered there aren't that many people out there who <u>think highly of</u> me. I've got an interesting, well-paid job and I'm <u>in good with</u> management, so as I see it now, <u>there's no question</u>. I'm staying.

55B. Read and fill in the blanks.

E-Memo to division managers:

From: Gridley[Nationalelectronics@Speedco.net]
Sent: Monday, September 24, 11:15AM
To: Janet Key, Ahn Ng, Herbert Polaski, Raj Gupta
Subject: Travel expenses

People,

   <u>There's no</u> _____ that our reps should live comfortably when they're abroad for us. But when it looks as if they're living ____ <u>off the hog</u>, they're just <u>sticking</u> ____ <u>to us</u>, and that's too much. They all <u>have</u> ____ <u>opinions of</u> themselves, and they're right—they all do good work. But I don't _____ <u>too highly of</u> the expense accounts they render. Victor, for example, has ____ <u>his disposal</u> in Chengdu a car and driver all the time that he's there like he's some kind of ____ <u>cheese</u>. I've <u>changed my</u> _____ , and don't intend to <u>foot</u> ____ <u>bill</u> for that kind of luxury. I have to stay <u>in good</u> ____ the chairman, and I know you want to do the same with me. Please help.

                                                                Gridley

110   The Idiom Book

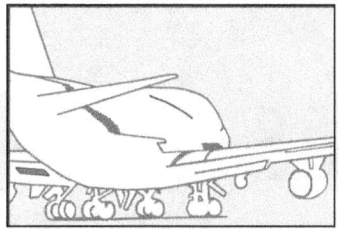

55C. Matching Exercise. In the parentheses write the letter of the meaning for each idiom.

Idiom

1) high off the hog ( )
2) foot the bill ( )
3) stick it to ( )
4) big cheese ( )
5) change one's mind ( )
6) have a good opinion of ( )
7) at one's disposal ( )
8) there's no question ( )
9) in good with ( )
10) think highly of ( )

Meaning

(a) to pay for something
(b) to treat badly; punish
(c) luxuriously
(d) important person
(e) to respect and admire
(f) to be well-liked by someone
(g) it's certainly true
(h) to make a new and different decision
(i) to think that someone or something is good
(j) available for someone's use

55D. Change each of the following sentences with an idiom from 55C.

1) He thinks he's pretty important. _____
2) Well?! he's living luxuriously. _____
3) They're really punishing the taxpayers. _____
4) And all the taxpayers pay for it, whether or not they like it. _____
5) The public treasury seems to be theirs to use. _____
6) I now respect and admire those who've been against it from the beginning. _____
7) I've made a new and different decision about this war. _____
8) Well, I don't think their work is any good. _____
9) I've got a wife and three kids, so I have to be sure that the boss likes me. _____
10) It's certainly true that the war is going badly. _____

The Idiom Book 111

Lesson 56

ENERGY CRISIS

56A. Read.

Harry: And our next guest on the *Harry at Ten* talk show is Professor Roger Rock of the National Energy Coalition. Professor Rock, welcome to the show. So, what's the <u>big deal</u> about fossil fuels?

Rock: Those are coal, natural gas, and petroleum (oil). They're residues of ancient life forms and we use them to produce heat, light, electricity, fuel, and lubricants. When they <u>come to an end</u>, and they will because they can never be replaced, modern economies will <u>come to a standstill</u> so today we have to do things to <u>bridge the gap</u>.

Harry: I assume there are competent people <u>in search of</u> new energy sources.

Rock: Yes, but <u>as yet</u>, what we'll replace the old ones with is <u>anybody's guess</u>.

Harry: So unless we really <u>get cracking</u>, it's going to <u>hit the fan</u>.

Rock: Crudely put, but <u>on the mark</u>.

56B. Read and fill in the blanks.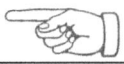

From: Jack Weiss <jweiss@amnet.com>
Sent: July 10
To: Mandy Brown <mandy500@wahoo.com>
Subject: Our friend Jenny

Dear Mandy,

  In our last exchange you asked about Jenny. Until November, Jenny had a thriving business delivering snacks from her boat to other boats on the river and to places on the shore. It was truly a ____<u>deal</u>—very profitable. It's effectively <u>come to</u>____<u>end</u> now because river traffic has <u>come</u>____<u>a standstill</u> with the arrival of fall. <u>As</u>____, she hasn't found anything to <u>bridge the</u>____ between now and the time she can resume delivery in the spring. She's <u>in</u>____<u>of</u> other sources of business but has found nothing yet, and it's <u>anybody's</u>____ when she will. It really ____<u>the fan</u> when the business stopped so suddenly, and she of course is anxious to ____<u>cracking</u> again. Regrettably, I was <u>on</u>____<u>mark</u> when I predicted this outcome.

                                                              Jack

112   The Idiom Book

56C. Matching Exercise. In the parentheses write the letter of the meaning for each idiom.

Idiom

1) big deal (   )
2) come to an end (   )
3) come to a standstill (   )
4) bridge the gap (   )
5) in search of (   )
6) as yet (   )
7) anybody's guess (   )
8) get cracking (   )
9) hit the fan (   )
10) on the mark (   )

Meaning

(a) to provide what is missing
(b) to stop functioning
(c) to stop existing; to end
(d) a very important matter or issue
(e) to start doing something as fast as possible
(f) something terrible happens
(g) exactly correct
(h) a mystery; something unknown
(i) so far; until now
(j) looking or searching carefully for something

56D. Change each of the following sentences with an idiom from 56C.

1) Trudy's graduation is a very important event. _____
2) The school year has ended, and it's now vacation time. _____
3) Traffic on the expressway stopped completely during the blizzard. _____
4) Until now, she hasn't found any business to replace what's missing. [Two idioms.] _____
5) She's looking for a new romance. _____
6) Whether he'll ever marry again is a mystery. _____
7) She's anxious to start working on her book full time again. _____
8) Some awful things are happening! I got fired, my car won't run, and the baby's got the measles. _____
9) She was quite right when she predicted that Jennie would have a huge success with her business. _____

Lesson 57
THE WINNING TICKET

57A. Read.

Mariko: <u>Guess what</u>—I won a car in the Star Dealer's raffle!

Yuko: Outstanding! You <u>can do with</u> some good luck <u>for a change</u>.

Mariko: Thanks. I'm already driving it. It will outstrip anything going, <u>stops on a dime</u>, and is the best car <u>on the road</u>. My husband thinks that it's going to be his car, but <u>he's got another think coming</u>. You know, <u>every so often</u> the price of gas <u>goes through the roof</u> because the refiners or OPEC decide to <u>put the screws to</u> the public; but with this car we'll <u>weather that storm</u> on one tank of fuel per month. Hah!

57B. Read and fill in the blanks.

From: Edward Fox <foxyEd@wondernet.com>
Date: August 25
To: Florence Fox <Flofox@SUV.edu>

Dear Flo,

    <u>Guess</u>____? Jake's dating a nice woman <u>for</u>____<u>change</u>, and he ____<u>do with</u> that kind of companionship. <u>Every</u>____<u>often</u> his boss <u>puts the</u>____<u>to</u> him—gives him the midnight shift for a couple of months from pure meanness, and Jake ____<u>through the roof</u> and almost gets fired. But with the help of a good woman, he'll be able to <u>weather the</u>____—when it happens again, as it will—without risking losing his job. (I hope.)
    In another area, the news is not so good: He's talking seriously of trying to buy a Belchfire Eight, one of the flashiest cars <u>on</u>____<u>road</u>. You know—it supposedly will go from a standstill to 100 in five seconds and then <u>stop on</u>____<u>dime</u>. I had thought that he was surrendering, little by little, to common sense, but I guess I <u>have</u>____<u>think coming</u>. I'm afraid our younger brother just won't grow up.

Love, Ed

114   The Idiom Book

57C. Matching Exercise. In the parentheses write the letter of the meaning for each idiom.

Idiom

1) stop on a dime ( )
2) for a change ( )
3) can do with ( )
4) guess what ( )
5) every so often ( )
6) have (got) another think coming ( )
7) on the road ( )
8) weather the storm ( )
9) put the screws to ( )
10) go through the roof ( )

Meaning

(a) to stop a vehicle within a very short distance
(b) finally
(c) to need (something)
(d) here's surprising and interesting news
(e) [1] to rise very high [2] to get very angry
(f) to force someone to do something by threatening
(g) to survive something hard or unpleasant
(h) occasionally
(i) to be mistaken, or wrong
(j) existing [of a vehicle]

57D. Change each of the following sentences with an idiom from 57C.

1) You won't believe this: I got the job! _____
2) This job is fairly demanding. I need a day off. _____
3) Good news: the sun is finally shining. _____
4) Her car's brakes are super—it stops within a very short distance. _____
  _____
5) I think Uncle Fudd drives one of the oldest cars still in existence. _____
  _____
6) You're quite mistaken if you think I'm going to lend him any more money. _____
  _____
7) Occasionally I have an overpowering urge to gorge on chocolate. _____
  _____
8) The price of gas went way up after the explosion at the refinery. _____
  _____
9) This new tax increase is really going to hurt low-income people. _____
  _____
10) This recession is rough, but we'll survive it. The house is all paid for. _____
  _____

The Idiom Book

Lesson 58
FACE TO FACE

58A. Read.

Sophia: Sometimes I wonder if my husband and I are communicating. <u>In essence</u>, we seem to be living in separate worlds.

Olivia: Yeah, I think that <u>the bottom line</u> is communication is a challenge even when people talk to each other <u>face to face</u>.

Sophia: My husband doesn't <u>get the drift</u> when I <u>let drop</u> that I might like to eat in a restaurant.

Olivia: <u>Welcome to the club</u>.

Sophia: You know, we wives are all <u>in the same boat</u>.

Olivia: Sometimes I think I'd rather <u>go it alone</u>.

Sophia: <u>Many's the</u> time I've thought the same thing. It's fairly easy for "communication" between a woman and a man to <u>go haywire</u>.

58B. Read and fill in the blanks.

Journal Notes, June 23

Yesterday I met <u>face</u> ___ face with Don Straight, a guy I'd only communicated with before in writing. I liked what he'd written for our EFL project in China, and I liked what I saw in his face. A good writer can conceal an unpleasant person, but the face can't, and Bill's face says that he's an honest sort, ___ <u>essence</u>, someone you can trust.

Bill's quite bright, but even I am too subtle for him, I guess. When I ___ <u>drop</u> that the chain restaurant we'd met in might be the wrong place to have lunch, he didn't <u>get</u> ___ <u>drift</u>. (So we suffered.)

Bill speaks Mandarin and I don't, and I don't want to ___ <u>it alone</u> in China, where too many things could ___ <u>haywire</u>. <u>Many's</u> ___ time a would-be entrepreneur has failed in China through ignorance, and I don't want anyone saying to me "<u>Welcome</u> ___ <u>the club</u>." <u>The bottom</u> ___ is if Bill and I are <u>in the same</u> ___ there, we might succeed.

58C. Matching Exercise. In the parentheses write the letter of the meaning for each idiom.

Idiom

1) the bottom line ( )
2) in essence ( )
3) get the drift ( )
4) face to face ( )
5) many's the ( )
6) go haywire ( )
7) in the same boat ( )
8) go it alone ( )
9) let drop ( )
10) welcome to the club ( )

Meaning

(a) to understand someone's meaning
(b) very close and looking at each other
(c) the final, most important point
(d) essentially
(e) to be alone and independent
(f) there's a lot more than one
(g) to start working or functioning improperly
(h) experiencing the same thing
(i) it's happened to a lot of us
(j) to divulge information

58D. Change each of the following sentences with an idiom from 58C.

1) This is essentially an administrative, not editorial, matter. _____

2) The result is we made a profit. _____

3) We were close together and she was looking at me and I at her. _____

4) I never did understand what she was hinting at. _____

5) She hinted broadly about her wedding plans. _____

6) So you got fired? Well, that's happened to everyone here. _____

7) We're all in the same situation. _____

8) I want to be alone and make my own decisions. _____

9) Several times I have tried to understand him. _____

10) My word processor often goes wild; it prints characters all over the page. _____

The Idiom Book 117

Lesson 59

COMMUTING

59A. Read.

Bill: Morning Joe. How was the commute?

Joe: For thousands of years our technical experts have been <u>making every effort</u> to find ways to move things through space ever faster, and we can now transport physical objects in spacecraft and transmit information in hyperspace.

Bill: So?

Joe: <u>The better to</u> ruin people's lives.

Bill: <u>That's as it may be</u>, my cynical friend, but <u>what's up</u> this morning? Why the <u>long face</u>?

Joe: My ultra-modern car is sitting in my driveway with a flat tire and that has <u>put a damper on</u> my spirits.

Bill: Oh, I can't blame you. As cars become <u>ever more</u> numerous, this increase <u>in turn</u> leads to ever more horrendous traffic jams and longer commutes. And as you're keenly aware, cars fail in <u>all kinds of</u> ways. I agree that they're a <u>mixed blessing</u>; they're fast, but they also cause a lot of problems. That's why I take the train.

59B. Read and fill in the blanks.

Journal: April 22 (Earth Day)

_____ <u>kinds of</u> environmentalists and experts have been <u>making</u> _____ effort to <u>put a damper</u> ____ our enthusiasm for gas-guzzling SUVs, _____ <u>better to</u> protect the planet, they claim. But despite those efforts, the monsters seem to be <u>ever</u> _____ popular and that, <u>in</u> _____, encourages the manufacturers to keep making them. So the tree huggers are wearing a <u>long</u> _____.

When reminded that the SUVs are not environmentally friendly, the gas and oil barons say, <u>that's as</u> _____ <u>may be</u>, but we have a duty to make money for our shareholders, and producing SUVs fulfills that duty and provides jobs. Thus, making the vehicles is not completely good or completely bad; it's a _____ <u>blessing</u>.

But I think it's a well-known fact that SUVs contribute to pollution, waste oil, and increase our dependency on foreign oil. And so I ask, <u>what's</u> _____ with the political leadership? Where's the energy policy? I should write to Representative Jefferson.

118   The Idiom Book

59C. Matching Exercise. In the parentheses write the letter of the meaning for each idiom.

Idiom

1) make every effort ( )
2) the better to ( )
3) that's as it may be ( )
4) what's up ( )
5) long face ( )
6) put a damper on ( )
7) ever more ( )
8) in turn ( )
9) all kinds of ( )
10) mixed blessing ( )

Meaning

(a) What's happening? What gives?
(b) perhaps
(c) so as more easily to; in order more easily to . . .
(d) to try as hard as possible
(e) consequently
(f) a lot of
(g) something both good and bad
(h) increasingly
(i) to lessen the intensity or enjoyment of (something)
(j) a disappointed or unhappy look on someone's face

59D. Change each of the following sentences with an idiom from 59C.

1) We should try as hard as possible to get people to vote. We *must* win this election. _____

2) We each have a cell phone, so as more easily to keep in touch. _____

3) "The court certified the election." "Perhaps, but it was still stolen." _____

4) What's happening at your house? _____
5) "Why are you so sad, Honey?" "My puppy ran away." _____

6) That awful news made a cheerful gathering a gloomy one. _____

7) The majority party is increasingly certain that it's running the country very well. _____

8) And the citizens are consequently feeling better. _____

9) My brother offers a lot of different reasons for not getting his homework done. _____

10) A word processor's both good and bad; it speeds writing, but a lot of time is wasted on getting the actual typescript to look the way you want it. _____

The Idiom Book 119

Lesson 60

ORGANIC OR

60A. Read.

Harry: Today our topic is food, and with us are Jim Howell of the Global Food Association, and Janet Fisher with Organics Now. Jim, tell us what your association is doing.

Howell: For one thing, thanks to our efforts, families in developed countries don't have to store food for long periods anymore because our commercial food distribution system processes and stores food <u>in bulk</u>, and the processing keeps it <u>fit to eat</u> all through the winter.

Fisher: Fit to eat? <u>No way</u>. It does <u>keep body and soul together</u>, but I have to <u>take issue with</u> your assessment of the quality, which <u>leaves a lot to be desired</u>.

Howell: <u>Point taken</u>, I suppose, and yeah, it isn't <u>home cooking</u>. <u>I stand corrected</u>. But you must admit that being able to buy in bulk and store for a long time <u>beats</u> running out of food <u>all to hell</u>.

60B. Read and fill in the blanks.

Journal
January 25—Mid-Winter Thoughts

We live pretty far from town and so we buy household goods ___ <u>bulk</u>—some food, cleaning supplies, etc. And the mail brings our newspapers and magazines. The cereal, pasta, beans, and rice are still <u>fit</u> ___ eat after six months—although the kids say "___ <u>way!</u>" to that— and we do manage to <u>keep</u> ___ <u>and soul together</u> with this system. I <u>take the kids'</u> ___ about the taste of the food sometimes, so I ___ <u>corrected there</u>; occasionally it ___ <u>a lot to be desired</u>. But I <u>take</u> ___ with their complaint that they don't get any <u>home</u> ___ . Maybe there's not a lot of variety in our meals, but our feeding routine <u>beats</u> being hungry <u>all</u> ___ <u>hell</u>.

PROCESSED?

60C. Matching Exercise. In the parentheses write the letter of the meaning for each idiom.

Idiom

1) in bulk ( )
2) fit to eat ( )
3) no way ( )
4) keep body and soul together ( )
5) take issue with ( )
6) point taken ( )
7) home cooking ( )
8) leave a lot to be desired ( )
9) I stand corrected ( )
10) beat . . . all to hell ( )

Meaning

(a) keep a person alive
(b) absolutely not
(c) edible
(d) in big amounts
(e) to be not good enough; be unsatisfactory
(f) I was wrong
(g) be a lot better than . . .
(h) plain, wholesome, good-tasting food
(i) I understand
(j) to disagree with . . .

60D. Change each of the following sentences with an idiom from 60C.

1) The cannery buys tomatoes in huge lots—four tons at one time. _____

2) Those potatoes are so old they're not edible. _____

3) You want to use the car again tonight? Certainly not! _____

4) I earn just enough to keep from starving. _____

5) She disagrees with the poll's analysis. _____

6) My brother-in-law's etiquette at table is far from polished. _____

7) I understand your feelings about that senator: I think he's a cheap crook, too. _____

8) I'd sure like a meal like one of those my mother made for me when I was little. _____

9) Yes, it's a lot more than 200 miles from Hamburg to Munich. I was wrong. _____

10) The food at Mother's Place is much better than the stuff at Chic City. _____

The Idiom Book **121**

Lesson 61

ADVICE

61A. Read.

Harry: Welcome to *Harry at Ten*. Our guest today is Mrs. Hortense Sage, noted advice columnist who has just turned 100. Hortense, what is your secret? What would you like to say to our listeners?

Sage: <u>Take it from me</u>: health is more important than anything else in life—love, money, fame, power . . .

Harry: But it's an unfortunate fact that starting life as a healthy baby is <u>out of your hands</u>.

Sage: Of course. But what you *can* control, at least partly, is the lifestyle you develop as a grownup. Vigorous daily exercise, plain food, and temperate—or no—use of drugs will <u>go a long way toward</u> keeping you <u>in good shape</u>.

Harry: And you are a perfect example that having useful, interesting work makes you feel good about yourself and about life, which does you <u>a world of good</u>.

Sage: Harry, you're so right. And people who claim to know what makes humans tick have discovered that friendship—affection—<u>plays a part</u> in keeping people healthy. Every adult knows that; we've all seen that people soured by life, and friendless, seem to die pretty young. Our understanding of the physics and chemistry of life helps us see why diet and exercise <u>make a difference</u> for human longevity, but we <u>don't have a clue</u> about why an intellectually active mind and agreeable emotions help keep the <u>Grim Reaper</u> <u>at bay</u>.

61B. Read and fill in the blanks.

> October 15
>
> Dear Arthur,
>
> I'm so sorry to learn about your accident. I hope you're doing OK. <u>Take it _____ me</u>: just as youth is wasted on the young, health is wasted on the healthy. Another friend of mine got in a terrible wreck three weeks ago, and now for the first time in his adult life what happens to him all through the day—what he does—is <u>out _____ his hands</u>, and he of course hates that. He's always been ___<u>good shape</u> and very active physically, and he <u>doesn't _____ a clue</u> how to cope psychologically with his physical helplessness. He's a little arrogant, and having to take orders from a 90-pound nurse will really do him <u>a _____ of good</u>; it'll <u>go a _____ way toward</u> making him more understanding of the weakness of others.
>
> Your physical courage will certainly <u>play a _____</u> in your recovery. Attitude does _____ <u>a difference</u> in these things, and you're definitely not ready to meet the <u>Grim _____</u>. With good luck and good care, you'll be able to keep serious diseases ___<u>bay</u> and live a long life.
>
> Reginald

122   The Idiom Book

61C. Matching Exercise. In the parentheses write the letter of the meaning for each idiom.

Idiom

1) take it from me ( )
2) out of one's hands ( )
3) go a long way toward ( )
4) in good shape ( )
5) a world of ( )
6) play a part ( )
7) make a difference ( )
8) not have a clue ( )
9) Grim Reaper ( )
10) at bay ( )

Meaning

(a) to be major factor in something
(b) healthy and physically fit
(c) believe me
(d) something that one cannot control
(e) a lot of; very much
(f) have an influence
(g) at a safe distance away
(h) death
(i) to have a important effect
(j) to have no knowledge or understanding

61D. Change each of the following sentences with an idiom from 61C.

1) Believe me, you'll never get a better offer. _____

2) I have no control over what happens to you now. _____

3) Her recommendation was a major factor in helping him get the job. _____

4) She looks great now: strong and healthy. _____

5) That quiet week at the lake did us a lot of good. _____

6) Her advice had some influence in their deciding to okay the project. _____

7) One's general attitude has an important effect on one's health. _____

8) He says he has no information about where the money went. _____

9) In his last hour he was serenely ready to meet death. _____

10) Old Wayne Vain is still trying, and hoping, to keep aging at a safe distance. _____

Lesson 62

REUNION

62A. Read.

Martha: So how are the reunion plans going?

Linda: They're arriving from <u>far and wide</u>. This'll be quite a reunion.

Martha: <u>Come on</u>—Uncle Fred from Osaka and Aunt Isabelle from Irkutsk?

Linda: <u>Honest to God</u>!

Martha: Great. But <u>God forbid</u> that Uncle Ralph should decide to come.

Linda: Let's hope. You know, when members of a family like ours gather at the <u>old stamping ground</u>, it can be a lot of work for us.

Martha: Yeah. People who've <u>long since</u> <u>moved away</u> tend to forget where things are, and as hosts we have to help them <u>get their bearings</u>. And there have been a lot of changes around here.

Linda: Uh-huh. And then they all sit around a table with drinks and listen to the grandparents <u>spin yarns</u> about <u>the old days</u>.

Martha: But it's worth it, isn't it?

62B. Read and fill in the blanks.

Diary: November 20

I looked ____<u>and wide</u> for my passport yesterday and complained to my roomie about not finding it, whereupon he snapped, "____<u>on</u>! It's right there on your dresser." <u>Honest</u> ____ <u>God</u>—sometimes I think that my memory's shot, and I'm only twenty five. _____ <u>forbid</u> I ever misplace my pants.

Last Sunday my high school graduating class met at our <u>old stamping</u> _____, Sotley's Tavern.

I had ____<u>away</u> from Springfield ____<u>since</u>, and at Sotley's I saw friends I hadn't seen in a long time; it was nice. It took me about five minutes to <u>get</u> ____ <u>bearings</u> again in Springfield, but of course I recognized my friends instantly. And it was fun to hear Bill ____<u>yarns</u>, as in ____<u>old days</u>, about all his old girlfriends. No one believes him now, either.

124 The Idiom Book

62C. Matching Exercise. In the parentheses write the letter of the meaning for each idiom.

Idiom

1) honest to god ( )
2) come on ( )
3) God forbid ( )
4) far and wide ( )
5) move away ( )
6) long since ( )
7) old stamping ground ( )
8) get one's bearings ( )
9) the old days ( )
10) spin yarns ( )

Meaning

(a) I hope it doesn't happen that . . .
(b) Truly!/? ; Really!/?
(c) I don't believe you
(d) places far away and widely separated
(e) to realize where you are or what your situation is
(f) to tell interesting, entertaining stories that are partly true
(g) the past
(h) to leave home and go to another place to live
(i) a long time ago
(j) a favorite gathering place in the past

62D. Change each of the following sentences with an idiom from 62C.

1) I get questions about my invention from all over the world. _____

2) You got an offer from Microsoft?! I don't believe you! _____

3) Really and truly: I did. _____
4) I hope to God my brother never gets sent to the war zone. _____

5) Mill Pond was our favorite skating place. _____
6) When the robbery happened, Rounder Ralph had been gone a long time, so he couldn't have done it. _____

7) I'm going to pack and go far away and never see you again. _____

8) The orienteering hikes taught me how to determine where I was in the woods. _____

9) I love to hear Uncle Spike talk about his days as an ironworker. I guess some of the stories are even true. _____
10) Grandma's tales about the past are fascinating. _____

The Idiom Book

Lesson 63

IN TRAINING AT

63A. Read.

Foreman: The woman I'm introducing you to trains all the new machine operators. She's not your boss, but while she's training you, <u>what she says goes</u>.

Trainee: How long will she be <u>looking over my shoulder</u>?

Foreman: Maybe a week. It depends on how long it takes you to <u>get up to speed</u>.

Trainee: I'm going to <u>break my back</u> to see that you keep me. I've got three kids.

Foreman: That's great because there's no <u>horsing around</u> here. When you're <u>on the job</u>, you work. There's no <u>goofing off</u>. You'll be <u>nine to five</u> during your training period. And be careful around <u>the opposite sex</u>; we've had a lot of sexual harassment charges here this year. If I hear any complaints, I'll be <u>on your back</u> in a minute.

63B. Read and fill in the blanks.

Okay, you recruits. Hear this: Corporal Harsh here is your training officer and <u>what he says</u>. He'll be <u>looking</u> <u>your shoulder</u> all through basic training; his job is to get you <u>up</u> <u>speed</u> here and he'll <u>break his</u> to do just that. You are to give him absolute, instant obedience or I'll be <u>your back</u> and you'll wish you were back home.

You're probably hoping you'll be <u>nine</u> <u>five</u> here, but in fact you're now <u>on</u> <u>job</u>, 24/7. There'll be no <u>horsing</u> when you're on duty. If there's any <u>goofing</u> you'll be sorry. And do be careful with members of <u>the opposite</u> : sexual harassment charges in the new army are not acceptable.

Good luck.

126 The Idiom Book

THE FACTORY

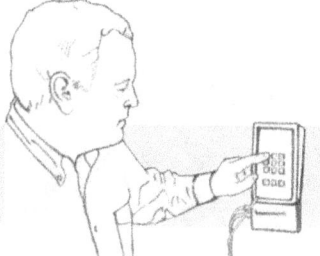

63C. Matching Exercise. In the parentheses write the letter of the meaning for each idiom.

Idiom

1) what one says goes ( )
2) look over someone's shoulder ( )
3) break one's back ( )
4) get up to speed ( )
5) horse around ( )
6) on someone's back ( )
7) nine to five ( )
8) goofing off ( )
9) the opposite sex ( )
10) on the job ( )

Meaning

(a) work as hard as possible
(b) become proficient in an activity or job
(c) to watch and control carefully
(d) one is in charge and must be obeyed
(e) giving someone a hard time
(f) working a day shift, (9:00–5:00)
(g) people of the other sex from you
(h) while working
(i) not working hard; wasting time
(j) to play boisterously, or scuffle, for fun

63D. Change each of the following sentences with an idiom from 63C.

1) I'm the boss here, and what I say here is the law. _____

2) She watches everything I do all day long. _____
3) Is Petey as good as the other kids yet in arithmetic? _____

4) No. But he's working very hard. _____
5) Quit playing around and get to work! _____
6) Firemen are available night and day. _____
7) Hey! Stop wasting time and get to work! _____
8) Claude works at the mill during the day shift. _____

9) He's 14 and has just discovered girls. _____
10) My new boss is giving me a hard time all day long. _____

The Idiom Book   127

Lesson 64
SALES MEETING

64A. Read.

Higley: Morning, people. We're here to get the "Fat No More" sales campaign <u>off the ground</u>.

Buncombe: Well, Chief, we've got <u>the green light</u> from distribution: there'll be half a million units <u>in stock</u> in grocery stores and drug stores three days after we <u>give the word</u>.

Higley: Thanks, Buncombe. Skinner, are the advertising people <u>in sync</u> with us on this?

Skinner: No. Everything's definitely *not* <u>in order</u>; I believe that using the word "fat" in the name of something we're trying to sell to fat people will offend them. We'll be <u>rubbing their noses in it</u>.

Higley: Lyon, you're running the project. <u>What's your take on</u> that?

Lyon: Well, <u>the whole shebang is in my hands</u>, and I'm telling you that if we make that kind of major change now, it'll be a financial and logistical disaster.

64B. Read and fill in the blanks.

From Cosmonaut Ivanov's Diary

I'm not sure that that damn spacecraft will ever <u>get</u> the ground. We got the <u>green</u> from the engineers all right, everything seems to be <u>order</u>, and all I have to do is <u>give</u> word, but . . .

It took us long enough to get <u>sync</u> with the admin people, but we finally have <u>stock</u> everything we needed to make sure of a properly provisioned flight. (I suppose mentioning their scheduling foul-ups to the director *was* <u>rubbing their</u> in it</u>, but they deserved it.)

I'm not sure I like having <u>the shebang on hands</u>; not when that entails guaranteeing the safety of a flight crew and I'm a bit uneasy about that safety. I'd like to say to Lomonovsky, "<u>What's your on</u> the situation?," but he's gone.

64C. Matching Exercise. In the parentheses write the letter of the meaning for each idiom.

Idiom

1) in stock ( )
2) the green light ( )
3) get off the ground ( )
4) give the word ( )
5) in order ( )
6) in sync ( )
7) on one's hands ( )
8) what's your take on ( )
9) the whole shebang ( )
10) rub someone's nose in it ( )

Meaning

(a) to issue an order
(b) available for use or for sale
(c) approval
(d) [1] to get (something) started [2] to fly
(e) what's your opinion of . . .
(f) everything
(g) as one's responsibility
(h) to keep reminding someone unnecessarily of his fault, shortcoming, or failure
(i) suitable; correct
(j) in accord or agreement

64D. Change each of the following sentences with an idiom from 64C.

1) The construction of the park never got started. _____
2) The city council never okayed the building of the park. _____
3) Have you got any rebuilt alternators available for sale? _____
4) As soon as you order us to do it, we'll erect the barricades. _____
5) This publisher's advertising and editorial units have a hard time working together harmoniously. _____
6) "Young lady, I think a change in your homework routine is necessary." "OK, Daddy." _____
7) The other kids keep taunting me about how bad my acting was in the school play. _____
8) Smedley, what do you think of her version of the accident? _____
9) They made me the stage manager for the school play: I'm responsible for everything. _____
10) No, I have to handle everything important: I'm the director. _____

Lesson 65

SNOW AND

65A. Read.

Marge: It's snowing pretty hard. I hope Clay <u>takes pity on</u> you and comes to help with his snowblower.

Bart: He'll probably be <u>up to his neck</u> with his own work. Besides, I can still use the <u>business end</u> of a shovel.

Marge: <u>Have it your way</u>. <u>For all I care</u>, you can use a spoon and shovel snow all day.

Bart: Hmm. We're <u>a bit</u> <u>out of sorts</u> this morning, aren't we?

Marge: Sorry. I'm <u>in the throes of</u> correcting final exams—I've been <u>hard at it</u> all week and I guess I'm getting snappish.

Bart: No—*I'm* sorry. I should have realized. Can I help in any way?

Marge: No, because you're not <u>up on</u> what they covered.

65B. Read and fill in the blanks.

From: Jane Rivers <janerivers@GreenGardens.com>
Date: March 23
To: Richard C. Rivers <richrivers@moneymatters.com>
Subject: Smells

Dick,

   Sorry to hear about your situation. Maybe your boss will <u>take pity</u> you and let you move your desk away from that guy who smells. Back here, I'm <u>hard</u> it trying to stock enough seed, saplings, and fertilizer for when spring finally arrives; and I must say that the smells in my greenhouse are better than the ones you apparently have in your office. I'm happily <u>up</u> my neck in new orders because of the weather change, and <u>for</u> I <u>care</u>, winter can never come back. (And I'm not so happily <u>in the throes</u> trying to keep our checking accounts in order.)

   My helper is getting reacquainted with the <u>business</u> of a spade: we're going to grow some saplings outside, not just in the greenhouse.

   If you think you must spend the money for that accounting course, <u>have it your</u> ; it's your career, and only you know what you have to do to succeed in that office. I guess I was snappish on the phone yesterday; I was <u>bit</u> <u>of sorts</u> about the cost of your course because I'd just paid a lot for the greenhouse supplies. Sorry.

   BTW You finance specialists are <u>up</u> the economic outlook: What's going to happen if we don't get a real energy policy?

Your Jane

---

130   The Idiom Book

FINAL EXAMS

65C. Matching Exercise. In the parentheses write the letter of the meaning for each idiom.

Idiom

1) business end ( )
2) up to one's neck ( )
3) take pity on ( )
4) have it your way ( )
5) for all I care ( )
6) out of sorts ( )
7) in the throes of ( )
8) a bit ( )
9) hard at it ( )
10) up on ( )

Meaning

(a) do as you please
(b) the part of a tool or weapon that does the work or causes the damage
(c) very busy
(d) to be kind and helpful to (someone who needs help)
(e) working very hard
(f) somewhat; a little
(g) aware or knowledgeable about (something)
(h) in the middle of (a hard or difficult situation)
(i) grouchy; irritable
(j) since I no longer care about it

65D. Change each of the following sentences with an idiom from 65C.

1) My teacher was kind and merciful: she gave me a passing grade. _____

2) He's been working hard in the garden all day. _____

3) Be careful with that knife: there's a vicious point on the tip. _____

4) Just do as you please; I know you don't care about my opinion, anyway. _____

5) You're cruel and thoughtless and, since I no longer care, go away and never come back. ____

6) She's a little older than he. _____

7) My husband's grouchy this morning. _____

8) Helen almost died during giving birth to their daughter. _____

9) Right now, I'm very busy with paperwork. _____

10) Do you know what's happening at the home office? _____

Lesson 66
DIPLOMACY

66A. Read.

Ava: How are you and Rob doing these days?

Sue: Like, not too good. He's angry at something I said. I guess I need some lessons in diplomacy.

Ava: Yeah. diplomacy is the art of <u>walking on eggshells</u>. It's being able to tell someone something disagreeable without offending that person.

Sue: Like, I need training in that art. My boyfriend <u>wouldn't give me the time of day</u> after I suggested, tactfully, that he might need a different mouthwash.

Ava: Yeah, I guess diplomacy isn't your <u>strong suit</u>.

Sue: I hate being <u>on the outs</u> with him because of this.

Ava: You two have had your <u>ups and downs</u> before; I'm sure you can handle this.

Sue: Well, he's very sensitive and also <u>set in his ways</u>; once he's <u>arrived at a decision</u> about something, that's it. When his feelings are hurt, as they are now, he <u>digs in his heels</u>, <u>turns a deaf ear to</u> my apologies, and ignores me. And he's <u>not about to</u> change.

66B. Read and fill in the blanks.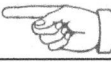

Diary

July 24

I <u>walked</u> eggshells all morning around Bill Blunt, who <u>wouldn't even give me the</u> of day. He and his wife have been ___ <u>the outs</u> for a long time, and last night she demanded a divorce. Like all married couples, they've had their share of <u>ups</u> <u>downs</u>, and I guess there were too many downs for her. Tact has never been his <u>strong</u> ___, and he's quite <u>set in</u> ways, so he's probably <u>arrived</u> a decision <u>to dig in his</u> and <u>turn a</u> ear to her requests and needs. But my guess is that now she's <u>not</u> to continue the marriage. I think he's lost her.

132 The Idiom Book

66C. Matching Exercise. In the parentheses write the letter of the meaning for each idiom.

Idiom

1) strong suit ( )
2) not give someone the time of day ( )
3) walk on eggshells ( )
4) on the outs ( )
5) dig in one's heels ( )
6) arrive at a decision ( )
7) set in one's ways ( )
8) ups and downs ( )
9) turn a deaf ear to ( )
10) not about to ( )

Meaning

(a) no longer friendly; arguing
(b) something that a person does well
(c) to ignore someone
(d) to be extremely careful not to offend someone
(e) to refuse to cooperate or change
(f) to refuse to listen to, or heed, someone
(g) determined not to or unwilling to (do something)
(h) unwilling to change one's habits or preferences
(i) to make a decision
(j) both good and bad experiences

66D. Change each of the following sentences with an idiom from 66C.

1) Be very careful not to get her mad or upset. _____
2) I greeted her this morning, but she completely ignored me. _____
3) The law firm of Crass & Gross is not very good at subtlety. _____
4) They've been arguing with their neighbors for months about that fence. _____
5) We've had both good and bad experiences over the last few years. _____
6) Grandma knows what she likes. Her motto is "My way, or the highway." _____
7) Have you finally decided what you're going to wear to the masquerade ball? _____
8) Mr. Strait refuses to change his mind; he will not vote for the gay-marriage proposal. _____
9) The boss flatly refused my request for a half-day on Friday. _____
10) She's decided, and she's definitely not willing to change her decision. _____

Lesson 67

WINTER FUN

67A. Read.

Bob: Hello, Dr. Torelli speaking.

Herb: Hi, Bob. This is Herb in Atlanta. How are you?

Bob: Fine, Herb, What's up? Still thinking about the position here at Northwood General Hospital? You know, you can really <u>have a ball</u> here in the north in January.

Herb: Yeah, sure. There are lots of <u>fun ways</u> to <u>risk life and limb</u>; you can <u>take a header</u> on skates, skis, or snowboards, <u>to say nothing of</u> icy city sidewalks

Bob: Yeah, but don't forget the ice fishing. All you need is a frozen lake, some simple equipment, some bait, and a box to sit on, and you're <u>in business</u>. You'll love it.

Herb: And snow and ice brings <u>all manner</u> of injuries: dislocated, broken, and cracked bones; frostbite; hypothermia; cuts; bruises; contusions, etcetera. I think I'd be in the ER 24/7.

Bob: Ah my friend—you <u>see the glass as half empty</u>.

Herb: Well, I don't <u>wear rose-colored glasses</u> and I guess that makes me a <u>wet blanket</u>, if that's what you mean.

Bob: Wet blanket or not, we'd love to have you up here in Northwood.

67B. Read and fill in the blanks.

> From: Kaitlyn North <kaitlynN@OLA.com>
> Date: June 20
> To: Elizabeth North <lizNorth.Lizgifts@NOVANET.com>
>
>   I went to a wedding reception last Saturday and really <u>had a   </u>. There was a pretty good band there; Uncle Fudd was trying to dance the tango and <u>took a   </u>, but he didn't hurt himself. Being around him on the dance floor is to <u>risk life and   </u>, but it's also lots of fun. A reception is a real, <u>   way</u> to see and mingle with family members, old and new.
>
>   Cousin Crabley was there in his usual persona of <u>   blanket</u>. He still likes to make it clear that he <u>sees the glass as half   </u>, in whatever situation, and he still can't be civil to family members, <u>to say   </u> of strangers. He's something else.
>
>   On a different topic: You know that I don't <u>see things through rose-colored   </u>, but I tell you that there are <u>all   of</u> new opportunities here with the new tech center opening. I'm pretty sure that if I offer my services to them as a tech consultant, I'll be <u>   business</u>.
>
>   Kaitlyn

67C. Matching Exercise. In the parentheses write the letter of the meaning for each idiom.

Idiom

1) take a header (　)
2) fun way (　)
3) risk life and limb (　)
4) have a ball (　)
5) wet blanket (　)
6) in business (　)
7) all manner of (　)
8) see the glass as half empty (　)
9) wear rose-colored glasses (　)
10) to say nothing of (　)

Meaning

(a) to fall headfirst
(b) to endanger one's life
(c) enjoyable activity
(d) to enjoy oneself immensely
(e) to be too sour, or pessimistic
(f) to be too optimistic
(g) someone who spoils other people's fun
(h) many different kinds of . . .
(i) [1] ready for some activity or process
　　[2] running a business
(j) and of course; or of course

67D. Change each of the following sentences with an idiom from 67C.

1) We had a grand time at Yuko's party. _____
2) Doing calculus homework is not an enjoyable way to spend the evening. _____
3) You do endanger your life if you use the freeway at rush hour. _____
4) Vickie tripped on a tug and fell head first this morning. _____
5) We could never afford the house alone or, of course, the house and the land it's on. _____
6) Get yourself a web site and you'll be all ready to talk and argue with the world. _____
7) Radio Hut always has numerous new electronic gadgets for sale. _____
8) Cousin Crabley always sees the worst side of things. _____
9) Marvin tends to see things quite optimistically, and he's often fooled. _____
10) With his sour personality, he often spoils other people's fun at a party. _____

The Idiom Book　135

Lesson 68

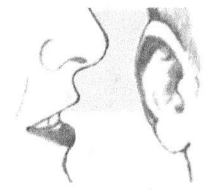

DIRTY TRICKS

68A. Read.

Daniel: Someone <u>played a trick on me</u> <u>the other day</u> and I <u>paid her back</u> immediately, <u>in spades</u>.

Joshua: Did it involve that Chinese girl you're <u>sweet on</u>?

Daniel: Well, uh, yes. It was her. She sent me a fake email message about my having won some lottery. When I discovered the hoax, I infected her PC with a mild virus. That is, I responded <u>with a vengeance</u>, and she deserved it.

Joshua: Cool! But <u>on the other hand</u>, she may <u>not give you a second look</u> now because I think you overreacted.

Daniel: <u>Of course</u>, I'm afraid of just that, but she'll <u>think twice</u> before she pulls that trick again, . . . and so will I before I react that way again.

68B. Read and fill in the blanks.

From: Carlos Lopez <carlopez.Smithall.VSU.edu>
Sent: October 31
To: Freddi Garcia <fred.Garcia@mspcc.edu>
Subject: Dirty (?) Tricks

Hey, amigo,

Tell me if I'm stupid.
<u>The</u> _____ <u>day</u>, a classmate of mine <u>played</u> _____ trick on me and I <u>paid</u> _____ back _____ spades, with _____ vengeance. She hid my car keys on me, and so I hid her *car* on her. She might _____ twice before she does that again. <u>On the</u> _____ hand, and _____ course, I don't want to really offend her because I'm <u>sweet</u> _____ her. She's brilliant, extremely nice, and very pretty, but right now at least she <u>won't give me a second</u> _____ as a potential boyfriend.
What do you think?

Carlito

136 The Idiom Book

68C. Matching Exercise. In the parentheses write the letter of the meaning for each idiom.

Idiom

1) the other day ( )
2) pay someone back ( )
3) play a trick on someone ( )
4) in spades ( )
5) with a vengeance ( )
6) think twice ( )
7) on the other hand ( )
8) of course ( )
9) sweet on someone ( )
10) not give someone a second look ( )

Meaning

(a) as fully as possible
(b) to trick someone for fun
(c) to get revenge on someone
(d) a few days ago
(e) obviously, certainly
(f) in love with someone
(g) to ignore someone
(h) however; though
(i) to hesitate, and think carefully
(j) forcefully, or extremely

68D. Change each of the following sentences with an idiom from 68C.

1) A few days ago, I saw the first robin of spring. _____

2) My sister tricked me yesterday: she tied the dog to my bed. _____

3) But I got back at her as much as I could: I put the cat in her dresser. _____

4) That storm last night arrived really violently. _____
5) He's in love with his English teacher. _____
6) She got revenge on her cheating husband: cleaned out the savings account and left town. __

7) She's quite green; however, she is bright and hardworking. _____

8) When she saw him at the party, she ignored him. _____

9) Naturally, I'll never do that again. _____
10) She paused and thought carefully, but then she did call him. _____

The Idiom Book 137

Lesson 69
WHO'S PAYING?

69A. Read.

Fran: David bought me dinner at Maxim's last night. For a long time I thought he <u>had something against</u> eating in public.

Lois: Hmm. I thought he had something against <u>parting with</u> a buck. I'd have guessed you two would <u>go Dutch</u>.

Fran: Oh, no. He's generous <u>to a fault</u>.

Lois: Maxim's is a pretty tony place. Were his <u>table manners</u> <u>up to the mark</u>?

Fran: Of course they were! You know, you still <u>hold it against him</u> that we beat you and Larry in that tennis match, but we took you <u>fair and square</u>.

Lois: Sorry. Larry and I have had a fight, and I guess I'm <u>taking it out on</u> you. And him.

Fran: I understand. I hope you two <u>patch things up</u> soon.

69B. Read and fill in the blanks.

A Page from the journal of <u>David C.</u>   Date: April 14

Took Fran to dinner last night at Maxim's. I think that maitre d' <u>had something</u> _____ me. Maybe my clothes weren't <u>up</u>   the mark; or perhaps it was my table _____. . . . Would Fran <u>hold</u>   against me if I suggested we ___ Dutch tomorrow? It's not so much that I hate to <u>part</u> _____ any of my hard-earned dough, but the fact is my checking account is pretty low . . . Fran's generous <u>to</u>   fault, so . . . yeah, but when I lost that argument with the supervisor, I <u>took it</u> _____ on Fran, and I hurt her. I'm so glad that we <u>patched</u> _____ up—she always plays <u>fair</u>   square with me, and I'm stupid for mistreating her. I don't deserve her. I guess I'll buy dinner tonight.

138 The Idiom Book

69C. Matching Exercise. In the parentheses write the letter of the meaning for each idiom.

Idiom

1) to a fault ( )
2) part with ( )
3) go Dutch ( )
4) have (got) something against . . . ( )
5) hold it against someone ( )
6) take it out on ( )
7) table manners ( )
8) fair and square ( )
9) up to the mark ( )
10) patch things up ( )

Meaning

(a) almost excessively; extremely
(b) to have a social event at which everyone pays their own way
(c) to lose, leave, or get rid of . . .
(d) to dislike . . .
(e) fairly and honestly
(f) to mistreat someone because of your anger against someone else
(g) to become friends again
(h) to be mad at someone because of something in the past
(i) acceptable
(j) the way you behave when eating

69D. Change each of the following sentences with an idiom from 69C.

1) That guy doesn't like me and I don't know why. _____
2) We hated to sell our old car. _____
3) Hyacinth and I stopped in that cafe, but we each paid for our own coffee. _____
4) I've got a good neighbor. He's almost too helpful. _____
5) Those little kids behave pretty well when they're eating. _____
6) The dean of students told me my grades weren't acceptable. _____
7) I dated her boyfriend a few times, and she's mad at me for that. _____
8) That old boss of mine was always honest and fair with me. _____
9) He lost his job, and now he's mad at me because of it. _____
10) The boys got into a fight, but now they're pals again. _____

Lesson 70
COLLEGE DORMS

70A. Read.

Britney: I have to share a room with another freshman, and the school didn't <u>see fit</u> to tell me about it <u>in advance</u>. Anyway, come over and inspect my new digs.

Rachel: OK. I'll be over <u>ASAP</u>. You're pretty lucky to get a room. I hear student housing's <u>in short supply</u> now.

Britney: Yeah, I heard unused dorm space has <u>pretty much</u> disappeared.

Rachel: I know <u>quite a few</u> students who are finding it really hard to <u>make it</u>. A lot of them have to find a place where they can easily go back and forth to classes <u>on foot</u>. And if a student <u>gets in bad with</u> her landlady, she's <u>between a rock and a hard place</u>; she can stay in an unpleasant atmosphere or leave with all her belongings and look for a new place.

70B. Read and fill in the blanks.

From: Jack Jones <jones.marketing@CRAssociates.com>
Sent: 9:55 A.M.
To: Jill Jones jill.sales@DowntownRealty.com
Subject: I didn't get it

Jill,

   Well, the company <u>saw</u> to promote Fawnley instead of me, and they didn't warn me <u>in   </u>. I'd leave here A AP if there were something suitable available, but good jobs are <u>in short   </u>; so, I'm <u>pretty   </u> stuck here.

   Don't worry—I'm not going to <u>get   bad</u> with management here because of my feelings about this. There are still <u>quite   few</u> good slots that will be opening soon, and I'll probably be able to get one of them. I don't intend to put us <u>between a   and a hard place</u>—economically—ever again. There are good things about this job: I can get to work <u>   foot</u>, so we save a lot of dough on transport. And we'd never <u>make   </u> without the company health insurance, for which thank God.

   See you tonight.

                                                                        Love,
                                                                        Jack

140   The Idiom Book

70C. Matching Exercise. In the parentheses write the letter of the meaning for each idiom.

Idiom

1) in short supply ( )
2) in advance ( )
3) ASAP ( )
4) see fit ( )
5) on foot ( )
6) make it ( )
7) quite a few ( )
8) pretty much ( )
9) get in bad with ( )
10) between a rock and a hard place ( )

Meaning

(a) not abundant; scarce
(b) very soon; quickly (as soon as possible)
(c) beforehand
(d) to decide it is correct or appropriate (to do something)
(e) by walking
(f) become disliked by someone
(g) forced to choose between two very bad things
(h) to survive
(i) a fairly high number
(j) almost completely; almost certainly

70D. Change each of the following sentences with an idiom from 70C.

1) She decided to change my work hours and didn't tell me about it beforehand. [Two idioms.] _____

2) OK. Tell the boss I'll be there in just a few minutes. _____

3) Boy—patience and good humor aren't very abundant in this office. _____

4) You can tell the boss I'm almost finished with the project. _____

5) A fairly high number of students did well on the test. _____

6) The doc tells me that if I don't have the operation, I might not survive. _____

7) "How will she get here?" "By walking." _____

8) If you're disliked by that professor, you'll have a terrible semester. _____

9) I have a difficult choice to make: a painful operation, or risk the cancer coming back. _____

The Idiom Book 141

Lesson 71
ACADEMIC ADVICE

71A. Read.

Advisor: As your academic advisor, let me give you some suggestions about being a successful student here at CSU.

Advisee: Cool. Lay it on.

Advisor: In the first few class sessions, try to learn what the instructors expect <u>in the way of</u> student response.

Advisee: <u>I take it</u> that asking questions is OK?

Advisor: Sure. In fact, <u>all other things being equal</u>, students who ask them get better marks than those who stay silent.

Advisee: Hmm. I <u>took it for granted</u> that the written assignments were much more important than class participation.

Advisor: No, no. Talk, and try to answer the instructors' questions in class. And don't <u>fall asleep</u> in class.

Advisee: OK. I'll try to talk <u>rather than</u> just <u>sit back</u> and listen.

Advisor: Good. If you do, you'll <u>get on the good side</u> of the instructors; and being <u>on good terms with</u> them means that you'll probably get <u>the benefit of the doubt</u> if your work is on the borderline between OK and not very good.

71B. Read and fill in the blanks.

Come on in and take a seat Mr. Hope. <u>I take</u> you are ready to begin work with us. What you expect <u>in</u> <u>way of</u> salary has already been settled, so a few comments about the work and about this company. The writer you'd replace had the habit of <u>falling</u> every morning around ten and waking around eleven; we <u>it for granted</u> that you wouldn't have that habit. There are no automatic raises here. <u>All other</u> <u>being equal</u>, the quality—not quantity—of a writer's work determines which writer is highest paid; the managing editor and I make that determination.

   We know of course that you wouldn't <u>back</u> and relax <u>rather</u> work. And if you want to get <u>on the</u> <u>side</u> of the administrative types here, be <u>on really good</u> with them—they run the place. Always give them <u>the benefit of the</u> when there's a difference of opinion concerning the accuracy of your pay, vacation, or insurance records; writers make as many mistakes as the admin types. Any questions?

71C. Matching Exercise. In the parentheses write the letter of the meaning for each idiom.

Idiom

1) all things being equal ( )
2) I take it ( )
3) in the way of ( )
4) take it for granted ( )
5) the benefit of the doubt ( )
6) rather than ( )
7) on good terms with ( )
8) get on the good side ( )
9) sit back ( )
10) fall asleep ( )

Meaning

(a) to assume . . .
(b) when there are no other important differences
(c) to assume
(d) with regard to; in the nature of; as
(e) become friendly with someone
(f) liked by, or friendly with, someone
(g) to be judged or treated favorably, not unfavorably
(h) to relax and make no effort
(i) and not; instead of
(j) to begin sleeping

71D. Change each of the following sentences with an idiom from 71C.

1) Just what can you show me as proof? _____
2) I assume you're leaving. Have a good life. _____
3) If there are no important differences in the quality of their work, they'll be paid the same. ___
_____
4) We assumed that you were a citizen. _____
5) Don't start sleeping during the director's speech. She wouldn't like that. _____
6) He intends to work in Khabarovsk instead of Irkutsk. _____
7) Those admin people relax and shuffle papers while we produce. _____
8) If you want to be friends with the principal, start by wearing your jeans higher. _____
9) Smarmley's liked by all the board members. _____
10) If someone does something that might, or might not, be dishonest, judge them kindly. We all make mistakes. _____

The Idiom Book

Lesson 72
BREAKING THE NEWS

72A. Read.

Kyle: Hey, sis, it's your little bro, Kyle.
Haley: Kyle. What's up?
Kyle: Well, Pop <u>hit the ceiling</u> when I told him I was leaving school.
Haley: I guess it really <u>took him by surprise</u>.
Kyle: Well, yeah. It <u>blew him away</u>, but he <u>has no idea</u> what college is like now.
Haley: Still <u>got your heart set on</u> joining the army?
Kyle: I joined last week. But <u>keep it under your hat</u>—Pop doesn't know that yet.
Haley: He'll think you've <u>flipped out</u>.
Kyle: Maybe. When he does hear, he'll probably think that Mom will <u>throw a fit</u> about it, so he'll want to <u>keep her in the dark</u> for a while before he <u>breaks the news</u> to her. But you know—she handles stress better than he does.

72B. Read and fill in the blanks.

From: Sue Nelson <Sue.personnel@Widget.inc.com>
Date: October 25
To: Kate Nelson <Katybird@Smithsonsinc.com>
Subject: Your friend Tess

Sister Kate:

When Gridley <u>broke</u> news about the new assignments, Neela <u>the ceiling</u>. It's not so much that she was <u>taken</u> surprise, but that she'd <u>had her</u> <u>set on</u> being the public relations deputy; now that's impossible. She was <u>blown</u> by Gridley's decision.

I'm not sure why Gridley <u>kept us</u> <u>the dark</u> about the reorganization. The president probably told him to <u>keep it</u> <u>his hat</u>, for his own reasons.

I <u>have</u> idea how well the new arrangement will work, but I'm not going to <u>throw a</u> over it and I won't <u>flip</u> because I don't own Widget Manufacturing, Inc.

Love,
Sister Sue

144 The Idiom Book

72C. Matching Exercise. In the parentheses write the letter of the meaning for each idiom.

Idiom

1) hit the ceiling (   )
2) take someone by surprise (   )
3) blow someone away (   )
4) have no idea (   )
5) have (got) one's heart set on (   )
6) keep something under one's hat (   )
7) flipped out (   )
8) throw a fit (   )
9) keep someone in the dark (   )
10) break the news (   )

Meaning

(a) to have no knowledge or understanding of . . .
(b) to shock someone
(c) to surprise (someone)
(d) to suddenly get very mad
(e) to become very angry and upset
(f) not give someone important or interesting information
(g) to tell what has happened
(h) become surprised and irrational
(i) to keep information secret
(j) to want very much to be or do something

72D. Change each of the following sentences with an idiom from 72C.

1) When Vickie told us about her marriage, it sure surprised us. [Two idioms.] _____

2) Minnie's mother got really mad; and she was shocked because her only daughter hadn't confided in her. [Three idioms.] _____

3) She'd planned, and wanted very much, to have a grand formal ceremony for Minnie. _____

4) I sure don't understand how Minnie managed not to tell anyone: she loves to blab secrets. [Two idioms.] _____

5) It must have been easy for Rod Ruhe, the groom, to stay silent: he's very antisocial. _____

6) Minnie's mom almost went crazy. _____

7) I don't think I'd be upset, if a 40-year-old daughter of mine finally got married, even suddenly and secretly. _____

Lesson 73

SPEEDING TICKET

73A. Read.

Wade: I was driving to Toronto <u>the other night</u>, and I got a speeding ticket.
Jeff: A ticket?—not even a warning?
Wade: Nah. I think she <u>has a thing</u> about anybody with a beard.
Jeff: Well, you do like to <u>put the pedal to the metal</u>. You <u>just plain</u> got caught, my friend.
Wade: <u>I tell you</u> she was <u>lying in wait</u> at an underpass. It was entrapment.
Jeff: Entrapment? <u>Bull</u>! You broke the law and got <u>caught in the act</u>.
Wade: Whatever. But I never got ticketed for speeding before. Once I got ticketed for not wearing a seatbelt, and that cost me <u>a pretty penny</u>. I tried to <u>talk my way</u> out of it then, and failed, and that happened this time, too.

73B. Read and fill in the blanks.

From: Paul D'Angelo <Paul@CB.Propertymanagement.com>
Date: 10:45 September 19
To: Pete D'Angelo <peterdangel@wahoo.com>
Subject: Meeting tomorrow re: Oakvale condos

Pete,

    Knowing you like to get up late, I'm telling you to <u>put the _____ to the metal</u> as soon as you get in your car if you don't want to be late for the meeting tomorrow. Basil ____<u>plain</u> hates it when people arrive late for his sessions; he <u>has</u> ____ <u>thing</u> about waiting. <u>The</u> _____ <u>night</u> before we left their house for the movies, he actually scolded his wife in front of Daisy and me because she kept us waiting for about five minutes. <u>I</u> ____ <u>you</u> he's pretty strange about that.

    As for the meeting about the condos, if and when we remodel the condos, it'll cost us <u>a _____ penny</u>. The plumbing and electrical contractors are just <u>lying in</u> _____, chuckling and rubbing their hands together. I'd prefer delaying the whole thing.

    By the way, that new admin assistant was looking at porn on her PC during lunch time today and I accidentally <u>caught her in</u> _____ <u>act</u>. She was totally embarrassed and tried to <u>talk</u> _____ <u>way</u> out of it, saying that it was on her machine when she got back from lunch and someone else must have logged on. Someone else . . . bull!

                                                                      Paul

73C. Matching Exercise. In the parentheses write the letter of the meaning for each idiom.

Idiom

1) the other night ( )
2) put the pedal to the metal ( )
3) have a thing about ( )
4) just plain ( )
5) a pretty penny ( )
6) lie in wait ( )
7) talk one's way ( )
8) catch in the act ( )
9) I tell you ( )
10) bull! ( )

Meaning

(a) simply and truly
(b) to have an unreasonable dislike of . . .
(c) to drive very fast in a vehicle
(d) during a recent night
(e) to catch someone doing something wrong
(f) a lot of money
(g) This is the truth:
(h) Nonsense!
(i) to hide and wait to catch or attack someone
(j) to persuade someone to allow you to do something

73D. Change each of the following sentences with an idiom from 73C.

1) Last Friday night I actually saw a UFO. _____
2) My grandfather has an unreasonable dislike of women TV news readers. _____
3) She loves to get on an empty road and drive that car as fast as it will go. _____
4) "You selfish brute. You simply and truly don't care." _____
5) This is the truth: She's impossible to live with. _____
6) My cat, Crackers, hid and watched for three hours, waiting for the mouse. _____
7) "He says he can run five miles." "Five miles? No way! He couldn't do five blocks." _____
8) We nabbed that guy as he was trying to hot-wire our car. _____
9) That car's a beaut; it must have cost a lot of dough. _____
10) She tried to sweet-talk the guard into letting her into the concert, but it didn't work. _____

Lesson 74

LUCKY?

74A. Read.

Dr. Perez: Good morning, Mr. Harris.

Harris: Morning, Doc. I'm here because a woman decided not to stop at a stop sign yesterday morning, and <u>ran into</u> me; now my right hip is <u>giving me fits</u>. Can you get it back <u>in working order</u>?

[Later.]

Dr. Perez: The X-rays don't show any damage.

Harris: That's good. I guess I'm lucky, <u>in a way</u>, because she might have hurt me a lot worse. I could even be <u>pushing up daisies</u>.

Dr. Perez: Well, you seem to be OK. I strongly recommend that you work with our physical therapist—she can <u>do wonders</u> with a hip like yours.

Harris: Yes, I guess I'm lucky, relatively; <u>all the same</u>, that gal's recklessness cost me <u>a nice piece of change</u>—a day's wages—because I never got to work yesterday. I know she'll never <u>make good on</u> my loss.

Dr. Perez: <u>Even so</u>, you're lucky: You're alive.

74B. Read and fill in the blanks.

September 5

A couple of nights ago I was backing my car into the garage and <u>ran</u> _____ the garage door. I was lucky <u>in a</u> _____, because I almost hit the dog; if I'd done so, it would now be <u>pushing</u> _____ <u>daisies</u>. Anyway, Uncle Ralph can _____ <u>wonders</u> with something like a door that won't close, and he'll soon have it back <u>in working</u> _____, as good as new; so there's no problem there. <u>Even</u> _____, my sister is <u>giving me</u> _____ about my need for driver training, and about how it would have cost me <u>a nice</u> _____ <u>of change</u> to get the door fixed if Ralph weren't around. I'll _____ <u>good on</u> what I owe her for harassing me by reminding her in public of the time she got that terrible sunburn on her butt. We compete and skirmish with each other all the time but, <u>all</u> _____ <u>same</u>, we love each other. We're sisters.

148 The Idiom Book

74C. Matching Exercise. In the parentheses write the letter of the meaning for each idiom.

Idiom

1) in a way ( )
2) run into ( )
3) in working order ( )
4) give someone fits ( )
5) pushing up daisies ( )
6) do wonders ( )
7) all the same ( )
8) a nice piece of change ( )
9) make good on ( )
10) even so ( )

Meaning

(a) in some respects
(b) working or functioning properly
(c) [1] to not function properly; be a problem [2] to kid, or irritate, someone
(d) to hit someone or something with your moving vehicle
(e) a lot of money
(f) to do or pay what you should as compensation, or because of a promise
(g) still; however; nevertheless
(h) dead
(i) to be good at solving problems
(j) nevertheless

74D. Change each of the following sentences with an idiom from 74C.

1) Nana was taking her walk yesterday when a kid on a bike hit her. _____

2) This word processor doesn't work right: it's driving me crazy. _____

3) Cousin Clyde helped me rehang the garage door and now it works right again. _____

4) In some respects, the promotion hasn't been so good: I'm no longer working with my old buddies. _____

5) My sister told me that old Uncle Fudd is dead. He was 93 years old. _____

6) A week at the cottage will help you a lot—physically and psychologically. _____

7) We got a big discount on our car; nevertheless, it cost us a lot. [Two idioms.] _____

8) Winnie still hasn't kept her promise to teach me the tango. _____

9) John got all As and Bs this marking period; but still, his year's average is pretty low. _____

The Idiom Book 149

Lesson 75

MORE THERAPY

75A. Read.

Walter: My physical therapist is <u>doing her damnedest</u> to get me <u>back on my feet</u>, and now we're finally <u>getting somewhere</u>.

Howard: Does she have you <u>jumping through hoops</u>?

Walter: Yes. And there's always something even harder <u>in the works</u> for the next session. Sometimes I want to <u>go for her throat</u> even though she's doing what I pay her to do.

Howard: <u>No pain, no gain</u>?

Walter: Something like that. But pain or not, I'm going to <u>stay the course</u>—it's working, and I'm making good progress.

Howard: Nice work! <u>Keep it up</u>.

75B. Read and fill in the blanks.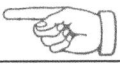

> From: Donald V. Persons, VP <VPPersons@CASTCO.COM>
> Date: January 24
> To: Department Heads: Alfredo Hernandez, Kazu Tomoko, Mary Stewart, Arthur Washington
> Subject: Thanks and Congrats to all
>
> Alfredo, Kaz, Mary, Art
>
>   I want to thank you all for <u>doing</u> damnedest to <u>get us back</u> our feet. I know you've been <u>jumping through</u> _____ to make us a serious competitor in the casting business again, and we now seem to be _____ <u>somewhere</u>: the purchasing chief for Ajax Motors called this AM and told me they've accepted our bid for those three million castings, so it's <u>in</u> works.
>   Good work, people! <u>Keep</u> up.
>   <u>Keep</u> mind that we have to <u>stay</u> course—maintaining excellent quality control and meeting production schedules. And if a foreperson sees two machine operators <u>go</u> each other's throat, those two are to be terminated immediately; we must have no labor problems. It won't be easy, but remember the well-worn cliche: <u>no pain, no</u> _____.
>
>   Persons

The Idiom Book

75C. Matching Exercise. In the parentheses write the letter of the meaning for each idiom.

Idiom

1) jump through hoops (   )
2) back on one's feet (   )
3) do one's damnedest (   )
4) getting somewhere (   )
5) no pain no gain (   )
6) keep it up (   )
7) keep in mind (   )
8) in the works (   )
9) stay the course (   )
10) go for someone's throat (   )

Meaning

(a) to do a lot of hard things in order to complete a process
(b) making progress
(c) [1] healthy and physically fit again [2] again functioning well professionally or financially
(d) to work or try as hard as possible
(e) progress requires pain or suffering
(f) to keep trying; not quit
(g) Good! You're doing well!
(h) not forget; remember
(i) to attack someone verbally
(j) coming in the future; planned

75D. Change each of the following sentences with an idiom from 75C.

1) We're doing everything we can to finish this job on time. _____

2) Liz is walking again. But that knee operation was a serious trauma. _____

3) Hah—now we're making progress. The city manager wants to talk about our proposal. _____

4) We've been doing a lot of various hard things to win the contract. _____

5) There's a big birthday party planned for Minnie. _____
6) The two candidates attacked each other savagely. _____
7) Remember that we have to get that bill paid by the first of the month. _____

8) A lot of personal trainers like to say if you don't work hard, you won't progress. _____

9) It takes terrific discipline and single-mindedness not to quit in a marathon race. _____

10) You're bringing in more and more orders. Good work. _____

Lesson 76
AT THE LEDGES

76A. Read.

Mark: Shall we <u>hang out</u> at the ledges today, and maybe even do some climbing? It's so nice out. And we could pick up Pete <u>on the way</u>.

Mandy: <u>Sounds like a plan</u>. I wonder if Pete's <u>got it in him</u> to go up over the ledges yet.

Mark: <u>I wouldn't count on it</u>. He can hike, but he still doesn't like to climb.

Mandy: OK. Let's <u>get going</u>.

Mark: Right. Time to <u>burn rubber</u>.

Mandy: You know, every time your nephew goes with us he always makes a mess and we have to <u>pick up after him</u>. I wish you'd <u>get on him</u> about that.

Mark: I'll <u>see what I can do</u>.

76B. Read and fill in the blanks.

This is Claude. I'm not in, so leave a message at the beep.

Claude, it's Hank. Bruce says he's going to stop at Richard and Hyacinth's <u>on</u> way here and <u>hang</u> with them. He'll stay overnight and get here tomorrow. I'll ask Richard to tell Bruce to <u>get</u> early tomorrow morning so he'll be here on time.

As to your picnic scheme—<u>sounds</u> a plan. I'll bring beer and chips. You know having Bruce at the picnic is no picnic. It's a two-mile hike into the lake and I don't think Bruce <u>has it</u> him to work that hard for some sandwiches. And he makes no effort to carry out his own litter. I'm tired of <u>picking up</u> him and I've got to <u>get</u> him about that. So, Claude, get here early tomorrow. I'll be ready to <u>rubber</u> at 9:30. And persuading Hyacinth to attend? <u>I'll</u> what I can do, but <u>I wouldn't</u> on it.

That's all for now. See ya.

152 The Idiom Book

76C. Matching Exercise. In the parentheses write the letter of the meaning for each idiom.

Idiom

1) on the way ( )
2) hang out ( )
3) have (got) it in one ( )
4) sounds like a plan ( )
5) I wouldn't count on it ( )
6) burn rubber ( )
7) get going ( )
8) pick up after someone ( )
9) see what one can do ( )
10) get on someone ( )

Meaning

(a) to have the ability to accomplish something
(b) I agree
(c) while traveling
(d) spend some time
(e) to pick up someone else's trash/junk/stuff
(f) to tell (strongly) someone to improve or change
(g) to try
(h) to leave, or go, fast
(i) to begin, or start
(j) I don't think so

76D. Change each of the following sentences with an idiom from 76C.

1) I'm looking forward to spending a few days at the lake. _____

2) We had to stop for gas while driving to the airport. _____

3) A picnic in the park? I agree! _____

4) Do you think she's really able now to leave that guy? _____

5) Hmm. I don't think so. _____

6) Hey—the parade starts in fifteen minutes. We should start. _____

7) We'd better get out of here right away. _____

8) I spend too much time cleaning the house when he finally leaves. _____

9) She reminded me all day about my promise to take that stuff to the dump. _____

10) Get your brother-in-law a job? Well, I'll try. _____

Lesson 77

MORE HEAT

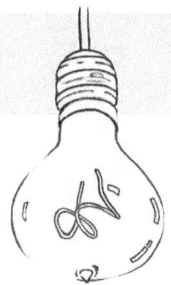

77A. Read.

Stella: I'm leaving! <u>What's more</u>, I'm not coming back.

Logan: <u>For crying out loud</u>—what's wrong? <u>What gives with you</u>, anyway?

Stella: I'm not tolerating any more of your lies and irresponsible behavior. <u>I've had it</u>.

Logan: OK, OK. So I didn't <u>keep my word</u> a few times. And, yes, I may have <u>broken a promise</u> a few times. But there's no need to <u>go ape</u>.

Stella: Right. I unreasonably and unjustifiably <u>go ballistic</u> over your *harmless and inoffensive* sophomoric stunts. Harmless and inoffensive because it's you that's pulling them.

Logan: Honey, please don't leave me. I promise I'll <u>turn over a new leaf</u>. How <u>on earth</u> could I survive without you?

77B. Read and fill in the blanks.

(a note of apology)

My dear Annie,

    When I said, "<u>What</u> _____ <u>with you</u>" and called you a witch, I was wrong. I promise to <u>turn</u> _____ <u>a new leaf</u>: I do mean to <u>keep</u> _____ <u>word</u> and not <u>break my</u> _____. I'm not surprised that you said you<u>'d had</u> _____ with me. I don't know how _____ <u>earth</u> I could _____ <u>ballistic</u> over having fish for dinner and be unconcerned about the possibility of not having you in my life. I'm deeply ashamed and sorry. <u>What's</u> _____, if you come back to me, I'll even learn how to cook fish! (Now, don't _____ <u>ape</u> over that; I won't do it every week. <u>For crying</u> _____ <u>loud</u>, I can barely find the stove; but I'll change, I will!)

All my love,

Bill

THAN LIGHT

77C. Matching Exercise. In the parentheses write the letter of the meaning for each idiom.

Idiom

1) what's more ( )
2) for crying out loud ( )
3) what gives with someone ( )
4) I've had it ( )
5) break a promise ( )
6) keep one's word ( )
7) go ballistic ( )
8) go ape ( )
9) turn over a new leaf ( )
10) on earth ( )

Meaning

(a) I'm thoroughly disgusted, and unwilling to tolerate this situation any more.
(b) what's the problem?
(c) I'm surprised, or upset, and a little bit annoyed
(d) and also; in addition; furthermore
(e) to become extremely upset
(f) to behave better and become nicer
(g) [Used to emphasize a question word.]
(h) to become very excited or angry
(i) not do what you promised to do
(j) to do what you promised to do

77D. Change each of the following sentences with an idiom from 77C.

1) Norton, you're fired. You're constantly late; furthermore, you've become unreliable. _____

2) Tom! Other people are waiting to use the toilet, you know. _____

3) Nana's in a very upset state. What's Grandpa done? _____

4) I'm fed up and thoroughly disgusted with your lame excuses. You're fired. _____

5) She gave me her word that she'd pay me back within a month, and she did. _____

6) He promised to pay her back within a month, but he didn't. _____

7) They got really mad when they saw the scratches on the car. _____

8) The girls are all wild about that handsome new coach. _____

9) Cousin Clyde is trying to change—to become a better person. _____

10) Where, oh where, did I put my car keys? _____

The Idiom Book 155

Lesson 78

BIG MOUTH

78A. Read.

Maria: I put my foot in my mouth Sunday when I was talking to Joan: I told her I had seen her husband, Terry, with Lola, an old girlfriend of his, the night before. You know, Joan and Terry are separated and both are consulting divorce lawyers. Then I asked her if the divorce was final yet. She then told me that she and Terry had been talking about reconciling, but now that she knew about Terry and Lola, she *would* get the divorce. I should have bitten my tongue; my big mouth got the best of me. I tried to tell her that there was nothing to *know* about the two, but she wouldn't listen.

Angel: Hmm. That's not like you, to spill the beans.

Maria: Well, I did; I let the cat out of the bag, even though there in fact *was* no secret.

Angel: I guess what you have to try to do now is convince her that the whole thing is much ado about nothing—a tempest in a teapot.

Maria: Of course. But that'll be far from easy. She knows her own mind.

78B. Read and fill in the blanks.

Journal Date: December 10

I often put my _____ in my mouth when I offer friends advice on matters I know little about. My _____ mouth got _____ best of me last week when I advised an old friend about buying a house. The prices of houses in a tract that my firm is handling were going to rise about 5 percent, and I spilled the _____ about that to my friend and suggested that a house there might be a good investment if bought before the price rise. (I've been trying to curb my problem of talking before thinking, but doing that is far _____ easy.) I'm going to try harder now to learn to _____ my tongue when I should: I'm in trouble with the law and at work because I let the _____ out of the bag concerning the price rise. I'm trying to persuade the law and my firm that divulging the price information was an innocent lapse and that their concern amounts to much _____ about nothing—a _____ in a teapot, but they don't seem convinced. Luckily, the bad advice this time hurt only me, not my friend.

I don't know what's going to happen, but I do know something about our local district attorney. She knows her _____ mind; she's not yet satisfied I'm blameless and is vigorously pursuing leads in the matter of my innocent lapse.

156 The Idiom Book

78C. Matching Exercise. In the parentheses write the letter of the meaning for each idiom.

Idiom

1) put one's foot in one's mouth ( )
2) bite one's tongue ( )
3) get the best of ( )
4) big mouth ( )
5) far from ( )
6) let the cat out of the bag ( )
7) know one's own mind ( )
8) tempest in a teapot ( )
9) spill the beans ( )
10) much ado about nothing ( )

Meaning

(a) to dominate or control (someone)
(b) a tendency to talk too much
(c) not talk although you want to
(d) to say something tactless or embarrassing
(e) a big unnecessary fuss about something unimportant
(f) certainly not
(g) to have clear, firm ideas and not be swayed by the opinions of others
(h) something minor that people get excited and upset over
(i) to divulge information inadvertently
(j) to tell a secret

78D. Change each of the following sentences with an idiom from 78C.

1) I guess I embarrassed him when I asked him if he'd found work yet. _____

2) He should have kept quiet; now he owes an apology to the senator. _____

3) His liking to talk so much gets him in trouble occasionally. _____

4) My urge to tell him a thing or two was just too strong. Now I'm in trouble. _____

5) Darn! Somebody told her about the surprise party. _____

6) I'm afraid I was the one who told her. _____

7) That frantic search for her missing money was a big fuss over nothing: she remembered she'd spent it at lunch. _____

8) That big uproar about the change in assignments was quite unnecessary: there were no changes. _____

9) It isn't easy to read the new boss. _____
10) It's not easy to get the boss to change her mind. _____

Lesson 79
MENDING FENCES

79A. Read.

Scott: The boss and I had a difference of opinion last week. <u>One thing led to another</u> and I foolishly <u>shot my mouth off</u>—intemperately.

Counselor: And now you're trying to get back in <u>his good graces</u>.

Scott: Exactly. But he's a <u>good sort</u>. He's always willing to <u>look the other way</u> when I <u>screw up</u>, as I often do.

Counselor: And so you hope he'll <u>put</u> your outburst <u>down to</u> poor judgment, and not faulty character.

Scott: Yes. I think If I acknowledge, <u>out loud</u>, that I'm <u>a nut case</u>, it'll be <u>over and done with</u>.

Counselor: I see. Now let's talk about why you think you are a "nut case."

79B. Read and fill in the blanks.

Diary

A couple of classmates of mine disagreed about something in gym class yesterday. Each one <u>shot his</u> _____ <u>off</u>, hollering became shoving, <u>one thing</u> _____ <u>to another</u>, and they finished by slugging each other. The coach stopped the fight and called them both, <u>out</u> _____ in front of a lot of other kids, stupid young thugs. It's all <u>over and</u> _____ <u>with</u> now; they're really pretty good buddies and they're back <u>in each other's</u> _____ <u>graces</u>. They both have fair records in school, and the vice principal is a _____ <u>sort</u> who's willing to <u>look the other</u> _____ when a bit of stupidity like this happens. He'll probably _____ it <u>down</u> to immaturity. But in fact the guy who started it is a real <u>nut</u> _____. He <u>screws</u> _____ all the time; he's a real trouble-maker who should be expelled.

158   The Idiom Book

79C. Matching Exercise. In the parentheses write the letter of the meaning for each idiom.

Idiom

1) one thing led to another ( )
2) shoot one's mouth off ( )
3) in someone's good graces ( )
4) a good sort ( )
5) look the other way ( )
6) screw up ( )
7) put something down to ( )
8) out loud ( )
9) a nut case ( )
10) over and done with ( )

Meaning

(a) [If you're *in* someone's *good graces*, that person approves of, or likes, you.]
(b) to talk carelessly or too much
(c) the situation was bad, and then it got worse
(d) someone who's pleasant and kind
(e) aloud
(f) finished; ended
(g) make a mistake
(h) to say or guess that the reason for something is . . .
(i) to ignore a minor flaw, misdeed, or infraction
(j) a mentally unstable person

79D. Change each of the following sentences with an idiom from 79C.

1) They bumped each other accidentally in the hall and said things they shouldn't have said, and then the situation got steadily worse and they got into a fight. [Two idioms.] _____

2) Min wants to be back on good terms with him, but I don't know . . . _____

3) My neighbor's a nice gal. She helps me whenever I ask her to. _____

4) The cops don't enforce the muffler regulations for motorcycles. _____

5) I'm very annoyed with myself; I made a huge mistake when I loaned my car to Lola. She brought it back on empty and with a dented fender. _____

6) I don't know why she acts that way. I ascribe it to ignorance. _____

7) Don't just shake your head. Tell me so that I can hear you, "Yes," or "No." _____

8) Helen and I don't agree on that guy: she thinks he's an eccentric artist and I think he's simply crazy. _____

9) Well, that love affair between Min and Bill has ended. _____

The Idiom Book 159

Lesson 80
TRIP TO THE BEACH

80A. Read.

Ali: Vanya—summer's here, and it's <u>high time</u> we took a drive down to the beach in your van.

Vanya: <u>No two ways about it</u>, Ali, but it's <u>against my better judgment</u> to take all you guys with me—but it *has* been a long winter. Let's go.

[Traveling to the beach.]

Ali: How far is it down there <u>as the crow flies</u>, Hidei?

Hidei: Around 90 kilometers. We must be <u>just about</u> there.

Vanya: It's <u>about time</u> somebody helped me drive. Hidei, when are you getting your license?

Hidei: <u>Any day now</u>.

[Driving back.]

Vanya: I need to take a break. Ali, can you take over.

Ali: Man, I'm <u>all in</u> from playing volleyball.

Vanya: Jorge? How about you?

Hidei: He's <u>sound asleep</u>.

Vanya: Thanks, guys. You know, <u>much as</u> I like to drive you guys around, how about at least helping with the gas?

80B. Read and fill in the blanks.

Journal   *Monday, June 13*

<u>No</u> ways about it: They're going to start construction of that mall across the road <u>any</u> now. So, <u>much</u> we hate the thought of moving from here, it's <u>high</u> we started making plans to do just that. Really, the paper says they're <u>just</u> ready to start excavating. It's <u>about</u> we got a two-bedroomer, anyway—Ruth's mother can't get a night's sleep on that couch when she visits. In fact, it's <u>against my</u> <u>judgment</u> to suggest this, but if her mother were living with us permanently, she could help with the rent. If we could get a place within a few minutes of the office <u>the crow flies</u>, it might be bearable.

I suppose it's the rigors of all this complex planning, but I'm <u>all</u>, and in a few minutes I'm going to be <u>sound</u>.

160   The Idiom Book

80C. Matching Exercise. In the parentheses write the letter of the meaning for each idiom.

Idiom

1) high time ( )
2) as the crow flies ( )
3) against my better judgment ( )
4) no two ways about it ( )
5) all in ( )
6) about time ( )
7) much as ( )
8) just about ( )
9) sound asleep ( )
10) any day now ( )

Meaning

(a) in a straight line [of distance]
(b) I think it may be a mistake...
(c) definitely; certainly
(d) it's now, or even later than the appropriate time
(e) sleeping
(f) tired; exhausted
(g) although
(h) quite soon
(i) it would be appropriate, even though overdue
(j) almost

80D. Change each of the following sentences with an idiom from 80C.

1) We should fix that leak before it gets any worse. _____

2) You have to be there tomorrow—definitely. _____

3) I think it may be a mistake, but I'm going to let you borrow the car. _____

4) The distance from here to New York City in a straight line is 250 miles. _____

5) She's almost ready. Give her a few more minutes. _____

6) I expected you guys to be able help me before now! _____

7) We'll be getting our first snow quite soon. _____

8) I'm tired. In a few minutes I'll be sleeping soundly. [Two idioms.] _____

9) Although I want to, I can't help you. _____

Lesson 81
FOREVER YOUNG?

81A. Read.

Marilyn: Charlie, <u>act your age</u>. That girl you were dancing with, if you call that dancing, is young enough to be your granddaughter.

Charlie: Man! First, I'm too old to dance, and then, to <u>add insult to injury</u>, I don't know *how* to dance. <u>At every turn</u>, my feelings are assaulted.

Marilyn: Oh my. <u>All of a sudden</u> we're mister sensitive.

Charlie: And <u>all at once</u> you're miz savage, <u>picking on me</u> again and again. I feel deeply wounded.

Marilyn: Really? Aah, you're <u>putting me on</u>. You know, <u>at times</u> I almost <u>take you seriously</u>.

81B. Read and fill in the blanks.

> From: Kelly Martin <u>KMartin2@northnet.com</u>
> Date: Saturday, March 18
> To: Caroline Scott <u>candbscott@calcom.net</u>
> Subject: Bill @ School
>
> Hi Mom,
>
> How goes it? We're all fine here, excepting Bill: his teacher doesn't seem to like him. <u>At every</u> _____ she'll tell him to <u>act his</u> _____ (He's 10!), or to start _____ his school work <u>seriously</u>, which he in fact does, or, <u>all</u> _____ <u>a sudden</u>, she tells him to stop writing and look at her—for no particular reason. To <u>add</u> _____ <u>to injury</u>, she gives him poor grades in English, and he's better at it than she is. One of Bill's real problems, ironically, is that, at the age of ten, he's already fairly proficient at <u>putting her</u> _____, and Bill's obvious intelligence and wit unsettle her. (<u>At</u> _____ I think she's somewhat intellectually challenged.) He can be answering a question of hers soberly and seriously and, <u>again</u> _____ <u>again</u>, inadvertently says something so outrageously funny that the whole room, including the teacher, howls. Then <u>all</u> _____ <u>once</u> he's in trouble again. I wish she would stop <u>picking</u> _____ <u>him</u>. Any advice?
>
> Kelly

162 The Idiom Book

81C. Matching Exercise. In the parentheses write the letter of the meaning for each idiom.

Idiom

1) at every turn (   )
2) add insult to injury (   )
3) act one's age (   )
4) all of a sudden (   )
5) again and again (   )
6) at times (   )
7) all at once (   )
8) put someone on (   )
9) pick on someone (   )
10) take someone/something seriously (   )

Meaning

(a) continually
(b) to be even unkinder or meaner to someone
(c) suddenly
(d) to behave as someone your age should behave
(e) purposefully mislead someone
(f) occasionally
(g) to consider important; treat with respect
(h) repeatedly
(i) suddenly
(j) tease or bother someone

81D. Change each of the following sentences with an idiom from 81C.

1) Laura, stop acting like a kindergartener. You're ten years old! _____

2) He pays a lot in alimony, and what's worse is that he's only allowed to see his daughter once a week. _____

3) I'm thinking seriously of quitting this job. The boss criticizes my work continually. _____

4) We were driving through a blinding rainstorm and suddenly it stopped and the sun shone again. _____

5) We were sitting there at the kitchen table talking, when suddenly the lights went out. _____

6) That big bully likes to push Jim around and make him feel bad. _____

7) She reminds him repeatedly of his responsibilities to her. _____

8) Uncle Ralph is very good at making us believe tall stories. _____

9) Sometimes I just want to run away. _____

10) I listen to the governor carefully when she gives a speech; she's worth listening to. _____

Lesson 82
RISKY BUSINESS

82A. Read.

Mei: I saw you walking <u>back and forth</u> on the sidewalk. What were you thinking about?

Morris: Well, I've had something <u>in the back of my mind</u> for a while that I'd like to talk to you about. I don't want to begin anything important <u>behind your back</u>.

Mei: OK, let's hear it. <u>Bend my ear</u>.

Morris: Ever since I lost my job at Enronoco—and isn't it great to see the CEO <u>behind bars</u>—I was thinking we could start a language school in Taiwan. With your Chinese and your experience in academia and my business background, it could succeed.

Mei: Hmm. I like the idea. But <u>in light of</u> all the competition already out there and no end <u>in sight</u> for the China-Taiwan question, is this the best time to start a business in Taiwan?

Morris: I think that unrest and uncertainty are "normal." When in historical times has the world ever been <u>at peace</u>? Sure we might <u>bite off more than we can chew</u>. <u>Without question</u>, starting a business is risky. So's life.

82B. Read and fill in the blanks.

> From: Bill Williams <u>billywill@dynanet.com</u>
> Date: January 23
> To: La Xiao Ping <LaPing5@SuperCom.net>
> Subject: Our future and China
> Dear La,
>   When I see the pendulum of the old wall clock swinging <u>back</u> _____ <u>forth</u>, it's a graphic reminder for me of the time that our crooked ex-CEO is going to spend <u>behind</u> _____. That guy was working busily <u>behind our</u> _____ stealing everything ___<u>sight</u>, looting the firm of *millions* of dollars, but he finally <u>bit off more</u> _____ <u>he could chew</u> when he got so greedy that he became careless about concealing the thefts. He's _____ <u>question</u> one of the greediest men in the world. But he got caught.
>   I've had something <u>in the</u> _____ <u>of my mind</u> that I'd like to _____ <u>your ear</u> about: It's an idea for making money, but honestly. Maybe we should think about trying to invest in a Chinese car-making company, or in a Chinese steel manufacturer. <u>In light</u> ___ their obvious intention, and ability, to become a major economic power fast, and with millions and millions of their people getting prosperous enough to be serious consumers, China's <u>without</u> _____ the most inviting—if riskiest—investment prospect there is. Let's think about it.
>   Bill

82C. Matching Exercise. In the parentheses, write the letter of the meaning for each idiom.

Idiom

1) in the back of one's mind (   )
2) back and forth (   )
3) bend someone's ear (   )
4) behind someone's back (   )
5) at peace (   )
6) in light of (   )
7) without question (   )
8) behind bars (   )
9) bite off more than one can chew (   )
10) in sight (   )

Meaning

(a) to talk to someone about something important
(b) secretly, so that the person does not know
(c) vaguely but persistently in one's thoughts
(d) forwards and backwards, repeatedly
(e) not fighting a war
(f) to try to do more than you are able to do
(g) of course; certainly; definitely
(h) in prison
(i) available
(j) because of; considering

82D. Change each of the following sentences with an idiom from 82C.

1) The tree branches were waving wildly in the wind. _____

2) For the last couple of years I've been thinking about moving to Canada. _____

3) That sneak is always talking about me secretly with my neighbor. _____

4) If you could spare me the time, I'd like to discuss a couple of serious issues with you. _____

5) He spent five years in prison for selling narcotics. _____

6) Because of all the snow, we postponed the trip to Grandma's. _____

7) A developer is buying all the land that he can around the lake. _____

8) When countries there aren't fighting a war, western Asia can be a splendid area to visit. _____

9) Poor Bill: he tried the impossible when he challenged Eric to a fight. _____

10) She's definitely the most stunning woman I've ever seen. _____

The Idiom Book   **165**

Lesson 83
CABIN FEVER

83A. Read.

Eve: You know, it's only late February, but I'm getting <u>cabin fever</u>.

Bob: <u>Same here</u>. Let's both <u>call in sick</u> and go snowshoeing.

Eve: <u>Hold it</u>—let's not <u>go overboard</u>. If I stayed out another Monday, I'd really <u>get it</u>, and rightly so.

Bob: Hmm. It's not like you to <u>get cold feet</u>, even in the winter (ha ha).

Eve: Ha ha yourself. It's not cold feet, it's a need for common sense and common courtesy. This outfit's been good to me and I intend to stay <u>on their good side</u> and <u>play the game</u>.

Eve: And I guess that would also be <u>playing it safe</u>.

83B. Read and fill in the blanks.

Charlie,

    I don't want to wake you up, so before I leave for work I'm *writing* to you. I can't see or hear you, but I know what you're thinking, and just <u>hold   </u>, Charlie. Don't <u> overboard</u>. I know it's the season for <u>   fever</u>, but if you <u>call   sick</u> and go to Aruba now, you'll really <u>get </u>; you might even get fired. If you told me that five months of winter makes you jumpy, I'd say, "<u>   here</u>," of course. I know it's easy for me to say this, but just <u>play   safe</u>, please. <u>Play   game</u> and stay <u>on their   side</u>. I know you're a risk taker, but I do hope you'll <u>get   feet</u> about sneaking away to the Caribbean. This is one risk we shouldn't take.
Think about it.

                                          Love,
                                          Marie

The Idiom Book

83C. Matching Exercise. In the parentheses, write the letter of the meaning for each idiom.

Idiom

1) call in sick ( )
2) same here ( )
3) cabin fever ( )
4) hold it ( )
5) get it ( )
6) go overboard ( )
7) play the game ( )
8) play it safe ( )
9) get cold feet ( )
10) on one's good side ( )

Meaning

(a) stop; wait
(b) to phone a work place and say you're sick and can't report for work
(c) I agree
(d) the feeling of a need for change or escape because of having been confined to one place for a long time
(e) to be friendly with someone
(f) to be honest; obey the rules
(g) to be careful, and take no risks
(h) to become nervous or afraid to do something
(i) to be scolded or punished
(j) to be too eager, enthusiastic, or impulsive; act hastily and rashly

83D. Change each of the following sentences with an idiom from 83C.

1) I sure don't like being stuck in this little house from November to April. _____

2) "This has been a long, hard day. I'd like a cold beer." "So would I." _____

3) If you call and tell your boss you're too sick to go to work, she might ask you for a note from your doctor. _____

4) Wait: that's the wrong road. _____
5) She usually overdoes the Christmas decorations. _____

6) My brother skipped school Monday, and his teacher and the principal both really scolded him. _____

7) Don't worry about being nervous and afraid to rappel. Everybody's afraid the first time. _____

8) If you can get the middle managers to like you, you'll do very well. _____

9) While you're in the army, just obey the rules, and you'll be OK. _____

10) Look—that country's almost in chaos. Be careful and don't take any unnecessary risks while you're there. _____

The Idiom Book 167

Lesson 84

FURNISHED

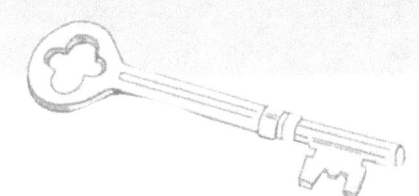

84A. Read.

Maria: So, Yuko, what else do we need for our apartment?

Yuko: Well, these boards might <u>come in handy</u> in the room. And <u>come to think of it</u>, we also need hooks for the kitchen and bathroom.

Maria: <u>I'm with you</u> there. The quality of the furnishings in our so-called furnished apartment isn't <u>all it's cracked up to be</u>. At least we're close to campus.

Yuko: Yeah, and the students and the faculty are cool. They're <u>beyond question</u> the <u>cream of the crop</u>.

Maria: <u>You've got that right</u>. Hey—do you want to get <u>a bite to eat</u>? I'm really hungry.

Yuko: <u>Me too</u>. Want to <u>chance it</u> at Mother Ransidd's?

84B. Read and fill in the blanks.

> MEMO
>
> TO: Division Chiefs   Date: 3/30
> FROM: A.C. Carter   RE: Various updates
>
> I'm sure you're all pleased that we're bringing on some computer help.
> Our new computer techie will <u>come in   </u> in this office. The "Help" part of the word processor isn't <u>what it's   up to be</u>; the explanations just aren't very good. Ms. Sharp's references say that she's the <u>cream of the   </u>; it's <u>   question</u> that we need help with word processing and the spreadsheets, so she should earn her money.
> On another note, I missed breakfast this morning so right now I could use <u>a bite   eat</u>. And <u>come to think   it</u>, maybe a company cafeteria is another addition we need. If enough of you division chiefs respond "<u>I'm   you there</u>," or "<u>   too</u>," we'll discuss it at the next meeting. We *are* adding ten machine operators, remember.
> And Rusakovsky, when you say that the Caspian gas fields are especially inviting now that China and India are actively hunting secure energy sources, <u>you've   that right</u>. It's time to <u>chance   </u> in Kazakhstan, so renew your passport and apply for a Kazakh business visa.

168 The Idiom Book

APARTMENT

84C. Matching Exercise. In the parentheses, write the letter of the meaning for each idiom.

Idiom

1) come in handy ( )
2) I'm with you there ( )
3) come to think of it ( )
4) not all it's cracked up to be ( )
5) chance it ( )
6) a bite to eat ( )
7) me too ( )
8) cream of the crop ( )
9) you've got that right ( )
10) beyond question ( )

Meaning

(a) not as good as people say it is
(b) I agree
(c) I've just remembered, or realized:
(d) to be useful
(e) lunch or light meal
(f) I feel, or think, the same way; same here
(g) to take a risk
(h) you're right; you're correct
(i) the best individual(s) in a group
(j) unquestionably; definitely; certainly

84D. Change each of the following sentences with an idiom from 84C.

1) This lumber might be useful at the cottage. _____

2) Now I remember: she's coming in tonight, not tomorrow. _____

3) If you think drilling there will be productive, I agree with you and support you. _____

4) Hmm. This program is not as good as people say it is. _____

5) She's unquestionably the best IT techie in the college. _____

6) Anne Louise is the very best of the lot. _____

7) If you've come to the conclusion that they really know what they're doing, you're right. ___

8) Is there anything in the fridge? I need something to eat. _____

9) So do I. _____

10) That diving board's pretty high. Do you want to take the risk? _____

Lesson 85

ELECTION

85A. Read.

Kevin: Hi, Brian. It's Kevin.
Brian: Hey, Kevin. What's up?
Kevin: I'm curious. Who's going to get the votes in your part of the state?
Brian: That <u>dark horse</u>, Newman, is getting a lot of response to his TV ads.
Kevin: He must have a supporter with <u>deep pockets</u>. He runs a new ad every week.
Brian: Oldham's been hinting darkly that Newman has a <u>skeleton in his closet</u> that should be disclosed to the voters as a public service.
Kevin: If I were an Oldham adviser, I'd tell him <u>not to go there</u>. I <u>know for a fact</u> that Oldham <u>did time</u> on a DUI charge about ten years ago, and if that <u>came to light</u>, he'd be a <u>dead duck</u>.
Brian: But he's an old-time politician, and you know <u>a leopard can't change its spots</u>. Look for some dirty politics.
Kevin: And <u>you can't teach an old dog new tricks</u>.

85B. Read and fill in the blanks.

From: Jacob Smart <jake.smart@walproducts.com>
Date: Monday, September 19
To: Lola Allbright lola.allbright@walproducts.com

Dear Lola,

    So you're the <u>dark</u>_____ competing for division chief?! Good luck. I <u>know</u>_____<u>a fact</u> that Feeley wants it, too, but he's got a <u>skeleton in his</u>_____ he wouldn't want to <u>come</u>____<u>light</u>: a couple of sexual assault charges. (He's never _____<u>time</u> for them.) I don't think he's a serious competitor anyway because he has all the charm of a public toilet. And he's probably already a _____ duck; the board members will have assessed his record and reputation and said to themselves and to each other things like "<u>the leopard can't</u>_____<u>its spots</u>," and "<u>you can't teach an</u>_____<u>dog new tricks</u>," etc., etc.
    This company has <u>deep</u>_____ and when you get the promotion—I think you will—they'll probably be paying you more than you deserve! J And about the situation between Vickie and me—<u>don't</u>____<u>there</u>.

                                                                 Best,
                                                                 Jake

85C. Matching Exercise. In the parentheses, write the letter of the meaning for each idiom.

Idiom

1) dark horse ( )
2) deep pockets ( )
3) not go there ( )
4) skeleton in one's closet ( )
5) come to light ( )
6) you can't teach an old dog new tricks ( )
7) know for a fact ( )
8) dead duck ( )
9) a leopard can't change its spots ( )
10) do time ( )

Meaning

(a) don't talk or ask about that
(b) an embarrassing or shameful secret from one's past
(c) the ability to help financially
(d) a contestant of unknown ability
(e) a hopeless loser
(f) people can't change their character
(g) old people don't like to learn new things
(h) to become known
(i) to serve a sentence in prison
(j) to know that it is true . . .

85D. Change each of the following sentences with an idiom from 85C.

1) We don't know how good a competitor that Japanese swimmer is. _____

2) The big defense contractors have plenty of money for the right political party. _____

3) There's something embarrassing in her past that she's very secretive about. _____

4) And if you're curious about my interview for that editing job, please don't ask. _____

5) I know it's true that she's been married twice before. _____

6) Uncle Ralph was once in a federal prison. _____

7) If news of that incident ever became known, she'd be lionized by the left and vilified by the right. _____

8) That so-called comedy show is a pathetic failure. It's being canceled. _____

9) Some people are born dishonest. They simply won't, and can't, change. _____

10) It's really hard to get old Uncle Fudd to try anything new. _____

The Idiom Book 171

Lesson 86
UNCLE RALPH

86A. Read.

Julia: Mom, do you remember Uncle Ralph?

Audrey: Oh, yes. <u>One day</u> Uncle Ralph arrived at Grandma and Grandpa's farm and stayed for two years. Uncle Ralph swore a lot <u>at first</u>, but Grandpa told him to either <u>cut it out</u> or <u>hit the road</u>. Ralph <u>got the message</u>. Once Grandma heard him bragging to the kids about how he could <u>drink his pals under the table</u>, and Grandma said to him, "<u>Don't you dare</u> tell the kids stories like that!" Right after that, Grandpa <u>read him the riot act</u>.

Julia: Was Uncle Ralph really a <u>blood relative</u>?

Audrey: Oh yes. Grandma's <u>kid brother</u>.

86B. Read and fill in the blanks.

October 15

Dear J

   <u>One</u> _____ recently Helen called me to talk about Grandpa's will. She was hesitant <u>at</u> _____, but soon managed to ask me if I had _____ <u>the message</u> that I was adopted and not a <u>blood</u> _____. I told her I had and that I wasn't upset. She apologized over and over and then I <u>read her the riot</u> _____ about her guilt feelings concerning the will and told her to <u>cut</u> _____ out, because she didn't write the will, Grandpa did.

   I've got a meeting in Detroit on Thursday, so I have to _____ <u>the road</u> tomorrow morning. Some of the guys attending are the kind who like to go to a bar after the meeting and try to _____ <u>their colleagues under the table</u>. I think I'll forgo that exercise. And <u>don't</u> _____ <u>dare</u> feel bad because Grandpa didn't leave me anything. Grandpa and I were never very close and I expected nothing.

                                            Love,
                                            your _____ <u>brother</u>, H

86C. Matching Exercise. In the parentheses, write the letter of the meaning for each idiom.

Idiom

1) one day ( )
2) at first ( )
3) cut it out ( )
4) hit the road ( )
5) read someone the riot act ( )
6) drink someone under the table ( )
7) blood relative ( )
8) get the message ( )
9) kid brother ( )
10) don't you dare ( )

Meaning

(a) go away; leave
(b) stop doing that
(c) in the beginning
(d) on a day in the past
(e) to warn or scold someone severely or harshly
(f) someone related by birth, not by marriage
(g) a younger brother
(h) I forbid you to . . . ; I demand that you not . . .
(i) to drink more alcohol than someone else, but not get as drunk
(j) to understand

86D. Change each of the following sentences with an idiom from 86C.

1) She called me in the afternoon recently and talked about the will. _____

2) In the beginning I found the skiing lessons very hard. _____

3) Hey, kids. I don't like that screaming, so stop it. _____

4) We have to leave early tomorrow. It's a long trip. _____

5) That was a pretty blunt editorial. I assume the PM understood. _____

6) Old Aunt Mabel liked to claim that she could drink more than any damn ironworker and still stay sober. _____

7) I forbid you to use that language, young lady! _____

8) Their teacher scolded and threatened them severely about the naughty words on the board. _____

9) Aunt Jean married Uncle Bill; but Aunt Anne is a real relative—she's Mom's sister. _____

10) That guy? He's my brother. And he's younger than me. _____

The Idiom Book 173

Lesson 87
TABLE MANNERS

87A. Read.

Ralph: Susan, Emmy's <u>eyes are bigger than her stomach</u>. She never <u>cleans her plate</u>.
Susan: Come on, Ralph, she does eat almost <u>each and every</u> bite.
Ralph: Maybe, but I'm about <u>at the end of my rope</u> with her. She eats like a little pig.
Susan: She's <u>every bit</u> as neat as her brothers.
Ralph: Neat! <u>Every time I turn around</u> she's raiding the fridge and making a mess. We'll have to <u>keep an eye on</u> her.
Susan: <u>Easy does it</u>, Ralph. She's only six.
Ralph: Only six—huh! That little imp learned <u>early on</u> how to handle males—especially her father.
Susan: Uh huh. She's <u>got your number</u>.

87B. Read and fill in the blanks.

From: Martin Smith < mjsmith@netcast.com>
Date: Saturday, July 12
To: Rose Salz rosys222@netcast.com
Subject: Thanks, etc.

Rose,

    Boy—<u>my eyes were bigger</u> _____ <u>my stomach</u> yesterday. I thought I'd never _____ <u>my plate</u>. Thanks again. <u>Each</u> _____ <u>every</u> meal you prepare is a masterpiece, and <u>I've reached the</u> _____ <u>of my rope</u> trying to think of how to repay your kindness. Your food is <u>every</u> _____ as good as what Mom used to give us.
    And, since we're discussing food, <u>every time you</u> _____ <u>around</u> the prices have risen. I know that you have to <u>keep an</u> _____ <u>on</u> the state of your household accounts—you're feeding Paul, his brothers, and yourself—so I won't be freeloading anymore (for a while). Bless you. And <u>easy</u> _____ <u>it</u> on hauling laundry up from the basement; I saw you favoring your back yesterday. You *have* got four males in the house!
    I clashed with the new boss _____ <u>on</u>—the second day. He's a dork but I'll outlast him. <u>I've got</u> _____ <u>number</u>.

                                      Love,
                                       Your brother (like it or not)

87C. Matching Exercise. In the parentheses, write the letter of the meaning for each idiom.

Idiom

1) each and every ( )
2) clean one's plate ( )
3) one's eyes are bigger than one's stomach ( )
4) the end of one's rope ( )
5) early on ( )
6) have got one's number ( )
7) easy does it ( )
8) keep an eye on ( )
9) every bit ( )
10) every time I turn around ( )

Meaning

(a) the end of one's patience, strength, or endurance
(b) [Used to emphasize *every*.]
(c) eat all the food on one's plate
(d) you took more food than you can eat
(e) be careful, and gentle
(f) at the beginning of a long process, procedure, or development
(g) to know how to control, handle, or manipulate someone
(h) to observe, or watch, carefully
(i) continually; too often
(j) equally; just

87D. Change each of the following sentences with an idiom from 87C.

1) Nana's supper looked so good that I took more than I could eat. _____

2) Food costs money, Bill, so don't waste any of that. _____

3) All the team members gave money for the coach's present. _____

4) I just can't find a way to get my sister and her husband to reconcile. _____

5) She's just as smart as her sister. _____
6) Too often, she wants to borrow money from me. _____

7) Watch the kids while I go to the store. _____
8) Don't be so rough. She didn't mean any harm. _____
9) Right at the beginning I knew this would be an interesting job. _____

10) Aha, you rascal, I see your strategy: You bluff! I can handle you. _____

The Idiom Book 175

Lesson 88
OFFICE SQUABBLE

88A. Read.

Tom: Well, Savage and Wilde are <u>on speaking terms</u> again. They've quit fighting <u>each other</u>, <u>for the time being</u> anyway.

Dick: They've <u>buried the hatchet</u>, huh?

Tom: Yeah. They've reached détente <u>yet again</u>. <u>Time was</u> a pair of battlers like those two would have been fired, but now they run the place.

Dick: <u>In my day</u> women weren't allowed to demonstrate that they could be as difficult and inept as men, but now there's equal opportunity in a lot more areas.

Tom: You know, the firm's doing pretty well, so it may actually be helpful that they don't <u>see eye to eye</u> on every issue.

Dick: Well, every time they fight <u>they give *me* a hard time</u>. I work directly for both of them and I always <u>get it in the neck</u> when they battle.

88B. Read and fill in the blanks.

From: Laura Johnson <EdandLaura@Southnet.net>
Date: Thursday, June 30
To: Alice Johnson <JFamily 50@Southnet.net>
Subject: Min and Bill

Hi Alice,

   Bad news. Min and Bill aren't __speaking terms—yet__. The awful truth is that they really do dislike __other__. I'll try to get them to __the hatchet__, <u>for</u> __time being__ anyway; otherwise the reunion will be tricky. Why do they find it so hard to <u>see</u> __to eye__ on so many things!? <u>Time</u> __family feuds were a bit more private. And __my day__ the family patriarch would have told those two to compose their differences. But now? Poor Bill, Min is always <u>giving him a</u> __time__ when something goes wrong in her little world; he always <u>gets it in the</u> __from her.

                                                                                Laura

176   The Idiom Book

88C. Matching Exercise. In the parentheses, write the letter of the meaning for each idiom.

Idiom

1) bury the hatchet ( )
2) for the time being ( )
3) each other ( )
4) on speaking terms ( )
5) yet again ( )
6) time was ( )
7) in one's day ( )
8) get it in the neck ( )
9) give someone a hard time ( )
10) see eye to eye ( )

Meaning

(a) to agree to stop arguing and become friendly again
(b) temporarily
(c) [If she likes him and he likes her, they like *each other*.]
(d) friendly enough to converse
(e) to agree completely
(f) make things difficult for someone
(g) to be punished harshly or severely
(h) when one was younger
(i) in the past; formerly
(j) for at least the third time

88D. Change each of the following sentences with an idiom from 88C.

1) They're friendly again and able to converse without immediately arguing. _____

2) I like her and she likes me. _____
3) That bandage will be OK temporarily. _____
4) They've agreed to stop quarreling and become friendly again. _____

5) Boy, Art flunked calculus, for at least the third time. _____

6) In the past she could climb that mountain in three hours. _____

7) When Grandma was young, there were far fewer cars. _____

8) The CEO and the president don't agree on the advisability of the merger. _____

9) When the boss makes a mistake, she yells at me. _____

10) He misbehaves a lot in school, and when that happens, he gets punished pretty severely. _____

The Idiom Book

Lesson 89
DIRTY WINDOWS

89A. Read.

Art: Bob, you'll have to use some <u>elbow grease</u> if you want to get those windows clean.

Bob: That <u>takes the cake</u>! Everybody's supposed to <u>do his part</u> here at the cottage. You're sitting on your butt and telling me that *I* have to work harder. <u>Where do you get off</u> talking to me that way?!

Art: I was just trying to <u>get a rise out of</u> you. I succeeded, huh?

Bob: If I <u>get hold of</u> a baseball bat, I'll show you how funny it was.

Art: OK, OK. You can <u>get even with</u> me at the poker table tonight. Maybe. If you can remember that a flush beats a straight.

Bob: <u>Get lost</u>. <u>Beat it</u>.

Art: Don't <u>beat around the bush</u>. Say what you mean.

89B. Read and fill in the blanks.

From: Robert Miller <rmiller25@wahoo,com>
Date: Saturday, September 12
To: B&HMiller<BnHMiller@castnet.com
Subject: Me and Mahmoud

My roomie, Mahmoud, and I really had to use <u>elbow</u> _____ to get our room useable. At first he refused to <u>do</u> _____ <u>part</u>, and then started offering suggestions about how I could clean *our* room faster and more efficiently, and that <u>took</u> _____ <u>cake</u>. I didn't <u>beat</u> _____ <u>the bush</u>; I asked him <u>where he</u> _____ off treating me as a servant, and told him to either _____ <u>hold of</u> a broom and go to work or _____ <u>lost</u> and find a new roomie. It worked. Maybe he was just trying to <u>get a</u> _____ <u>out of</u> me (which he did). And maybe he'll try to _____ <u>even with</u> me later because of my "insulting" him, but I think we'll be fine. He's a very intelligent Pakistani mathematician, and he's trying to teach me some Urdu. He had a woman friend over last Saturday and asked me to _____ <u>it</u> for the evening, which of course I did. We're starting to like each other.

178 The Idiom Book

89C. Matching Exercise. In the parentheses, write the letter of the meaning for each idiom.

Idiom

1) do one's part ( )
2) where do you get off [-ing . . .] ( )
3) elbow grease ( )
4) takes the cake ( )
5) beat it ( )
6) get even with ( )
7) get hold of ( )
8) get lost ( )
9) get a rise out of ( )
10) beat around the bush ( )

Meaning

(a) have no right (being or doing something)
(b) to do one's share of the work in a group effort
(c) is very bad (or very good)
(d) (more) physical effort; (more) energy
(e) go away
(f) go away
(g) to avoid saying something directly and clearly
(h) to get revenge against someone
(i) to grab or take in the hand; obtain
(j) to annoy or irritate someone purposely

89D. Change each of the following sentences with an idiom from 89C.

1) It'll take a lot of effort to get those spots out. _____

2) That's pretty bad. He pushes in front of me in the line then takes the last crab leg. _____

3) Grab a shovel, Pete, and do your share. We have to get this driveway cleared. _____

4) You have no right to give me orders. _____

5) He's so smug and self-satisfied—the other kids like to annoy him just for fun. _____

6) I grabbed his wrist and pulled him away from the saw. _____

7) When she left him, she broke his heart. He swore he'd get revenge. _____

8) Hey kid: get away from here—scram! _____

9) The time's getting short. I think I'd better scram. _____

10) Bruce, stop being so ambiguous. Speak plainly and say what you mean. _____

The Idiom Book 179

Lesson 90
EXPIRED LICENSE

90A. Read.

Ronald: Robert, once again <u>you're in hot water</u>. You'll have to <u>face the music</u>.

Robert: But, Dad, I wasn't <u>at fault</u>. That guy ignored the stop sign.

Ronald: But you were driving with an expired license. And when you're at the hearing, make sure you don't <u>lose your temper</u>. Don't go <u>flying off the handle</u>. Just <u>behave yourself</u>.

Robert: Don't worry. I'll be <u>the soul of</u> tact and discretion. <u>As usual</u>.

Ronald: <u>See that</u> you are.

Robert: <u>Your wish is my command</u>.

90B. Read and fill in the blanks.

> A Note from Johnny Jackson
>
> Frankie,
>
>   I was in a fight last night at the baseball game. I was __usual__ __fault__, because I __my temper__ and hit a guy. Now I'm in real __hot__ _____. I have to _____ __the music__ before a judge tomorrow morning. I admit that I <u>fly</u> <u>the handle</u> far too easily, and I intend in future to _____ __myself__ and be ____ __soul__ of temperance and restraint. No more fighting.
>
>   I'll have to ____ __that__ the guy's medical bills are paid, and that might be expensive.
>
>   I'm sorry. I hope you'll forgive me. If you want me to stay away a little while, <u>your</u> _____ <u>is my command</u>.
>
>   Johnny

180   The Idiom Book

90C. Matching Exercise. In the parentheses, write the letter of the meaning for each idiom.

Idiom

1) lose one's temper ( )
2) at fault ( )
3) face the music ( )
4) in hot water ( )
5) see that . . . ( )
6) your wish is my command ( )
7) the soul of ( )
8) fly off the handle ( )
9) as usual ( )
10) behave yourself ( )

Meaning

(a) to become uncontrollably angry
(b) guilty; responsible for something wrong
(c) to accept unpleasantness caused by your own mistake or misdeed
(d) there'll be trouble because of something that happened
(e) in the ordinary, predictable way
(f) my wish (or order) is . . .
(g) I'll obey all your wishes and commands
(h) someone who is a perfect example of . . . ; the embodiment of
(i) act properly and correctly; don't misbehave
(j) to become angry suddenly

90D. Change each of the following sentences with an idiom from 90C.

1) It's going to be bad now. The professor knows that we stole the exam. _____

2) I told you not to eat all the candy. Now you have to take your punishment. _____

3) She didn't stop, and she was responsible for the accident. _____

4) He got so mad that he lost control of himself. _____
5) Onslow, you often get too mad too easily. _____
6) Remember: a first grader should act properly and obey the teacher. _____

7) You should be a nice example of politeness and good manners. _____

8) He was late for work, in the usual, predictable way. _____

9) I'm ordering you to get home in time for supper. Don't stop at the pub! _____

10) Love, I'll obey all your commands. _____

The Idiom Book   181

Lesson 91
LEXICOGRAPHY

91A. Read.

[Rrrrring]

Kathy: Hi, Tiffany. How are things at Lexiconline Dictionary today?

Tiffany: Oh, Hi, Kath. Well, I was in trouble a little earlier this morning.

Kathy: Really? Over what?

Tiffany: Well, when the editor walked in this morning, he gave me <u>a dirty look</u>, marched into his office, came right back out again holding my definition of *contribution*, and <u>gave me a piece of his mind</u> about bringing politics into a dictionary definition. He was quite right of course.

Kathy: When you wrote that definition I suppose you were <u>blowing off steam</u> about all the sleaze and shadiness in the capital.

Tiffany: Yep. But I <u>made nice</u> with him. I <u>leaned over backwards</u> (for me) trying to apologize. I know as well as he does that politics is <u>off limits</u> in lexicography. But I <u>see red</u> when those hypocrites spout patriotism and piety publicly.

Kathy: So at least for now you're not <u>in the doghouse</u>.

Tiffany: Right. I have to go now. <u>Take care</u>.

Kathy: <u>See you</u>.

91B. Read and fill in the blanks.

> From: Charles Turbanian <ct.marketing@Roswellinc.com>
> Date: Tuesday, February 7
> To: Elizabeth Petrocelli <eliz.assistantVP@Roswellinc.com>
>
> Dear Lizzie,
>
>   Now that we're temporarily far enough away from each other that we can't begin exchanging gunfire, I'm <u>giving you a _____ of my mind</u> about that habit of yours of giving me a <u>dirty</u> _____ , in public, every time I express an opinion that offends you: cut it out. It really angers me. You shouldn't waste energy <u>blowing _____ steam</u> over how I like or don't like some actor or something like that. I do promise that I'll <u>bend _____ backward</u> to keep my opinions <u>off</u> _____ at the office. I don't want to be <u>in _____ doghouse</u> with you, honey. See, I'm _____ <u>nice</u>.
>
>   I appreciate that we all have our own likes and dislikes. I <u>see</u> _____ , for example, when I hear politicians brag that looting the public treasury is one of the great public services that they're performing.
>
>   I assume things are going well in Chengdu. _____ <u>care</u>. And regards to Qing Li. <u>See</u> _____ .
>
>   Love,
>   Charlie

91C. Matching Exercise. In the parentheses, write the letter of the meaning for each idiom.

Idiom

1) blow off steam ( )
2) give someone a piece of one's mind ( )
3) dirty look ( )
4) make nice ( )
5) see red ( )
6) see you ( )
7) in the doghouse ( )
8) take care ( )
9) lean over backwards ( )
10) off limits ( )

Meaning

(a) to be pleasant and agreeable to someone
(b) to express one's anger
(c) to tell a person that you are angry at her or him about something
(d) a glare
(e) in trouble
(f) goodbye [Informal]
(g) goodbye [Informal]
(h) to get very angry
(i) a forbidden area or topic
(j) to make a special effort

91D. Change each of the following sentences with an idiom from 91C.

1) Jenny glared at me when I mentioned how pretty Vickie looked. _____

2) When he again failed to finish his assignment punctually, I called him and read him the riot act. _____

3) Senator Flam expressed his anger at the media's treatment of the president. _____

4) The kids had a spat but now they're friends again. _____

5) Lola's in-laws are visiting, and she's making a special effort to be nice to them. _____

6) We're not allowed to talk about grandpa's girlfriend. _____

7) Grandma gets really mad when anyone mentions Vickie. _____

8) Now you're in for it—you put a dent in Mom's car. _____

9) You'll be here tomorrow, then? OK. Adios. _____

10) I have to catch that plane, guys. Ciao! _____

The Idiom Book   183

Lesson 92
THE LATEST BIG THING

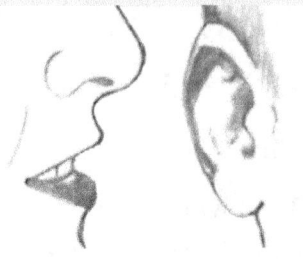

92A. Read.

Worker: Morning, Ms. Earnest. I apologize for the drowsiness; I <u>hardly ever</u> get up this early. Is there coffee <u>on hand</u>?

Ms. Earnest: <u>You bet</u>. I'll get you a cup.

Worker: <u>Tell you what</u>: I'll <u>help myself</u> if you can get me that latest report on the silicon-laser project.

Ms. Earnest: At the briefing yesterday, Mr. Newton said that he thinks they're <u>on to something</u>—that someday fairly soon they may get silicon to transmit data with light rather than electrons. That's pretty important.

Worker: <u>You're telling me</u>. You do appreciate, Ms. Earnest, that whatever you hear in this firm about the silicon-laser project must be <u>kept under wraps</u>?

Ms. Earnest: I handle *everything* that I learn here carefully. <u>My lips are sealed</u>. I <u>have no use for</u> blabbermouths.

92B. Read and fill in the blanks.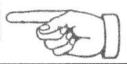

From: Joan Schmidt, PhD <JSchmidt.English@UVM.edu>
Date: March 31
To: Soraya Abdul <sorayaA.English@UVM.edu>

The midterm's ready, and I think the students are beginning to talk with each other in class, which they _____ <u>ever</u> did before last week. I'll be back from my trip in a week. Please <u>keep</u> everything about the midterm _____ <u>wraps</u>. And if Dean Sligh asks any questions, <u>your lips are</u> _____, right? You have to <u>handle</u> him carefully. I <u>have</u>____ use for that guy—he's a snoop. So <u>I'll tell you</u> _____: if he asks to see the midterm, tell him I took it with me and left no copy. About your comment regarding how hard it is to be civil to him: <u>You're</u> _____ <u>me</u>!

As for your request for leave for that wedding: <u>you</u>____; I'll authorize that before I leave. You know there's petty cash <u>on</u>_____—use it as you need it. And of course you're to _____ <u>yourself</u> to the coffee, doughnuts, whatever. But not your freeloading friends (please)!

By the way, I think you're ____<u>to something</u> with your analysis of Bergstrom's poetry.

92C. Matching Exercise. In the parentheses, write the letter of the meaning for each idiom.

Idiom

1) hardly ever ( )
2) on hand ( )
3) tell you what ( )
4) you bet ( )
5) help oneself ( )
6) on to something ( )
7) you're telling me ( )
8) keep under wraps ( )
9) one's lips are sealed ( )
10) have no use for ( )

Meaning

(a) here's a suggestion (or an offer):
(b) almost never
(c) available
(d) of course; certainly;
(e) to keep secret
(f) not tell anyone
(g) to have no respect for
(h) making progress with one's ideas
(i) take what you want; sure
(j) I already know and agree with that

92D. Change each of the following sentences with an idiom from 92C.

1) We almost never go to Chic City: it's too expensive. _____

2) There's a bit of money available for supplies. _____

3) Come to your wedding? Of course I will. _____

4) Here's a suggestion: If it doesn't work, call the tech center. _____

5) The food's ready kids—take what you want. _____

6) I think Brown has some good ideas. _____

7) Icy roads? I know—I went in the ditch this morning! _____

8) She's keeping her plans secret. _____

9) This is very important so don't tell a soul, OK? _____

10) I have no respect for liars. _____

The Idiom Book

Lesson 93

INVESTMENT

93A. Read.

Mike: Phil, we might be able to <u>make money hand over fist</u> if we <u>get in on the ground floor</u> of this Caspian gas deal.

Phil: Yes. As long as it exists, the gas might be selling <u>at a premium</u> because China and India have changed the energy picture.

Mike: Uh huh. I'd be <u>hard pressed</u> to think of a more attractive—if risky—opportunity. <u>In my book</u> we'd be crazy not to risk it. It<u>'s up to us</u>, you know, to try to make money for the stockholders.

Phil: Well, you know the <u>ins ands outs</u> of doing business in Almaty, and nobody else in the firm does, so <u>it stands to reason that</u> you should be the one to run the Caspian show.

Mike: Do you think the directors will be <u>in favor</u> of it?

Phil: In favor with <u>no ifs, ands, or buts</u>.

93B. Read and fill in the blanks.

Mike's Journal for December 31

New Year's Eve reflections: I wish I'd <u>got in</u> <u>the ground floor</u> of one of those successful Silicon Valley deals 15 or 20 years ago. They were _____ <u>money hand over fist</u>. Most of the dot-commers' "ideas" were flashy and worthless, but after the Net was developed quite a few clever people became millionaires.

The services of people who know the <u>ins</u> _____ <u>outs</u> of advertising on the Net are now selling ____ <u>a premium.</u> <u>In</u> ____ <u>book</u>, I'd be ____ <u>pressed</u> to think of a skill that's attracting more young people. Which major do you think more college freshmen are ____ <u>favor</u> of, one of the arts or computer technology? Computers, of course, <u>no ifs, ands, or buts</u>.

In the past it <u>was up</u> ____ colleges and universities to educate their students in the appreciation of literature, science, and the arts, but now the culture wants them to prepare students to make money. And unfortunately <u>it</u> _____ <u>to reason</u> that almost anyone would rather earn money than struggle with the poetry of Donne or Milton.

OPPORTUNITY

93C. Matching Exercise. In the parentheses, write the letter of the meaning for each idiom.

Idiom

1) make money hand over fist ( )
2) get in on the ground floor ( )
3) at a premium ( )
4) hard pressed ( )
5) in my book ( )
6) be up to ( )
7) ins and outs ( )
8) it stands to reason (that) ( )
9) in favor ( )
10) no ifs, ands, or buts ( )

Meaning

(a) almost unable
(b) at a high price
(c) to be a part of a business, activity, or plan from its beginning
(d) to make a lot of money fast and easily
(e) is quite clear, obvious, or logical
(f) supportive; agreeable; approving
(g) no reservations; no questions
(h) complex details
(i) a duty or obligation for someone
(j) it's my opinion (that) . . .

93D. Change each of the following sentences with an idiom from 93C.

1) Boy, they make a lot of dough fast and easily in the casino. _____

2) Yes, I'd like to be part of that dot-com right at the beginning. _____

3) Right now petrol is selling at a high price. _____

4) I'm almost unable to find a buyer for my old car. _____

5) In my opinion, those "patriots" should all be in jail. _____

6) It's the duty of a civilized government to help the helpless. _____

7) She understands the complexities of working with the regulatory agency. _____

8) It's logical that he wouldn't want to stay in that job: he has no chance for advancement. _____

9) They all favor the suggestion. _____

10) They support the proposal without any questions. _____

The Idiom Book   187

Lesson 94
KEEP YOUR SHIRT ON

94A. Read.

Jacob: It's <u>just as well</u> that we canceled the trip. There's a strike at the airport.

Ethan: <u>Just the same</u>, I'd sure like to see those people again.

Jacob: How can you say that with <u>a straight face</u>? You and Deirdre had a <u>knockdown-dragout</u> argument just before we left.

Ethan: The truth is, I hope desperately that we can <u>kiss and make up</u>.

Jacob: Well, <u>keep your shirt on</u>. Maybe we can go there in October. On the other hand, maybe you should <u>keep your distance</u>.

Ethan: And maybe you should <u>keep your nose out of my business</u>.

Jacob: Sorry. I promise to <u>keep my mouth shut</u>. I guess that I, <u>of all people</u>, with my two divorces, should not be giving any advice about women to anyone.

94B. Read and fill in the blanks.

From: Judy Drake <Judy.drake@CSBA.com>
Date: Tuesday, April 6
To: Jacob Ashkenaz <jacobathome@supercom.net>
Subject: War in the office

Jake,

    I hope you're enjoying your vacation. It's <u>just as</u> you weren't here yesterday. Cortez and Wright had a <u>knockdown-</u> argument about minority hiring. Cortez asked Wright when it was really going to begin and Wright told him to <u>keep his</u> <u>on</u>, that it would start at "the proper time." Wright told us all, with <u>a</u> <u>face</u>, how he'd always been a friend of minorities, and that's when things got hot. I don't think those two will <u>and make up</u> any time soon. That Wright, <u>of</u> <u>people</u>, should <u>keep</u> <u>mouth shut</u> about his views on diversity. I suggest you try to <u>keep your</u> from those two when you get back. It was pretty ugly.

    You might think I'm too interested in your affairs, and if you tell me to <u>keep my nose out</u> <u>your business</u>, I'll understand. I just don't want you to be unaware of what's been happening.

    But you know, this is a great place to work, <u>just</u> <u>same</u>. Good pay and interesting work, and we produce good stuff.

                                          Judy

94C. Matching Exercise. In the parentheses, write the letter of the meaning for each idiom.

Idiom

1) just the same ( )
2) just as well ( )
3) knockdown-dragout ( )
4) with a straight face ( )
5) keep one's distance ( )
6) of all people ( )
7) kiss and make up ( )
8) keep one's nose out of another's business ( )
9) keep one's mouth shut ( )
10) keep one's shirt on ( )

Meaning

(a) vicious
(b) with an unsmiling face
(c) nevertheless
(d) probably a lucky coincidence
(e) don't interfere
(f) not talk, or express opinions
(g) especially; definitely; certainly
(h) to stay safely away from someone or something dangerous
(i) don't become impatient
(j) settle an argument and become friendly again

94D. Change each of the following sentences with an idiom from 94C.

1) It was a lucky coincidence that we didn't go to that dinner. The restaurant lost all its power for the whole evening. _____

2) They don't pay very well. Nevertheless, the job's so interesting that I'd take it if they offered it to me. _____

3) She's 45? How can you say that without smiling? She's no more than 30. _____

4) Mabel and Bill had a really vicious argument about his "business" trip to Las Vegas. _____

5) They've been sweethearts for a long time, but I'm not sure they'll ever settle this argument. _____

6) Hey, don't be so impatient. We're doing this as fast as we can. _____

7) We've got to stay safely away from that fire. _____

8) Don't interfere in my personal affairs. _____
9) Don't tell anyone. Don't say anything. _____
10) We definitely didn't expect to see *you* here. _____

Lesson 95
DEATH AND TAXES

95A. Read.

Matt: Have you heard? Tom Riche <u>kicked the bucket</u>.

Kevin: <u>Six feet under</u>, eh? He'd <u>had one foot in the grave</u> for a long time and was about ready to <u>give up the ghost</u>, and the bankruptcy was probably just enough to finish him.

Matt: <u>Could be</u>.

Kevin: He should have <u>known better than</u> to invest all his dough in that casino scheme before it had been approved.

Matt: Those gambling promoters lied and lied and fooled him, and <u>left him holding the bag</u>. I wonder if he left any relatives to inherit the mess.

Kevin: <u>Let me see</u>. I think he has a son over in Ontario.

Matt: Well, if there is one, he should <u>leave well enough alone</u> and not even communicate with the courts because he might have to pay his father's debts.

Kevin: Yeah. Dealing with a bankruptcy administrator is <u>no laughing matter</u>.

95B. Read and fill in the blanks.

> From: Peter Adams <P.Adams.09@DuxburyPrep.edu>
> Date: Wednesday, October 19
> To: Randolph Adams <Adams@Adamsbakerclay.com>
> Subject: Dear Dad,
>
> The pressures of life in a boarding school are <u>no</u> _____ matter. The other day I thought I had scarlet fever and was close to being <u>six</u> _____ under. Really, I ____ <u>one foot in the grave</u>, and was ready to <u>give</u> _____ <u>the ghost</u>. Truly. No exaggeration. But as you see, I'm writing this note, so I didn't <u>kick the</u> _____. <u>Could be</u> that I was more lonesome than I was sick. I'll <u>leave</u> _____ <u>enough alone</u> and stop whining. (I <u>know better</u> _____ to expect sympathy from you.)
>
> <u>Let me</u> ____. What else has happened? Oh yes. Friday afternoon we were told to sweep the gym after basketball practice, but the other guys all sneaked away and _____ <u>me holding the bag</u>. But don't worry about me. I'll make it.
>
> I miss you all.
>
> Petey

95C. Matching Exercise. In the parentheses, write the letter of the meaning for each idiom.

Idiom

1) kick the bucket (   )
2) six feet under (   )
3) give up the ghost (   )
4) have one foot in the grave (   )
5) could be (   )
6) know better [than] (   )
7) leave well enough alone (   )
8) no laughing matter (   )
9) leave someone holding the bag (   )
10) let me see (   )

Meaning

(a) be near death
(b) to die
(c) dead
(d) to die
(e) give me time to think
(f) not interfere or make changes
(g) a serious issue
(h) make someone totally responsible for the duties of a whole group
(i) to know that it is unwise or dangerous (to be or do something)
(j) maybe; it's possible . . .

95D. Change each of the following sentences with an idiom from 95C.

1) Uncle Ralph finally died. The old guy was 95. _____
2) Great Grandpa? No, he's been dead for ten years. _____
3) That old woman had been near death for years before she finally succumbed. _____
4) Grandpa had a stroke and died._____
5) "Do you think she'd go out with me?" "Hmm. Maybe." _____
6) You passed that cop on the expressway? You know it's unwise to do that! _____
7) We were all told to clean the place after the dance, but the others sneaked off and left me with all the work. _____
8) The way to Rock Island? Give me a second—I believe it's due south on 55. _____
9) Listen: if they lowered your taxes that much, don't ask for more. _____
10) A loss of power here in February can be a very serious matter. _____

The Idiom Book   **191**

Lesson 96
STORMY WEATHER

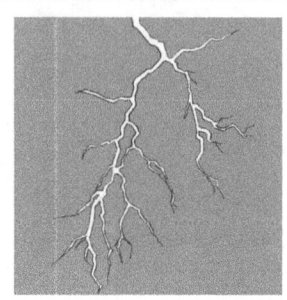

96A. Read.

Steve: Hi, Harry. We hear you've been <u>laid up</u>. How are you?

Harry: I'm fine now. But that storm that <u>laid waste to</u> the gulf coast destroyed all our property down there. Building and contents. <u>Lock, stock and barrel</u>.

Steve: That's awful. If you're <u>hard up</u> I can lend you a couple grand right now.

Harry: No, no. I'm OK. But thanks a lot for the offer. You really are <u>a friend in need</u>.

Steve: Are you going to try to <u>pick up the pieces</u> there?

Harry: If I thought I could <u>lay hands on</u> some building supplies right now, I'd accept your offer, but everything's been destroyed, including hardware stores and lumberyards. No. I'm <u>fed up with</u> life in the sunny south. I think I'll stay with the snow and ice <u>from here on out</u>.

Steve: Well, try to <u>bear in mind</u> that you and the family are safe, and that's what counts.

Harry: Amen.

96B. Read and fill in the blanks.

From: Randolph Scott <randscott@midcom.net>
Date: November 23
To: Tony Reed <AnthonyRandBess@midcom.net>
Subject: Enough is enough

Dear Tony,

　　You luckily missed the worst tornado that Bedny County has ever recorded. It <u>laid waste</u> most of the town's business section, and looters emptied the buildings still standing, <u>lock,</u> _____ , <u>and barrel</u>. The town was _____ up before the twister hit, and now I really don't know if it's going to be able to _____ <u>up the pieces</u>. There's no one to be <u>a</u> _____ <u>need</u> to this poor place.

　　By the way, because of her bad knee, Elizabeth was _____ up in the local hospital during the twister, which didn't touch the hospital. But she says that she's <u>fed</u> _____ <u>with</u> living in tornado country. (<u>Bear in</u> _____ that this was the twelfth one she experienced.) And <u>from here</u> _____ <u>out</u> I, too, am spending no more springs or summers in Twister City. As soon as I can _____ <u>my hands on</u> a train schedule, I'll be gone from the Great Plains.

Randolph

96C. Matching Exercise. In the parentheses, write the letter of the meaning for each idiom.

Idiom

1) lay waste to (   )
2) hard up (   )
3) lock, stock, and barrel (   )
4) laid up (   )
5) from here on out (   )
6) pick up the pieces (   )
7) bear in mind (   )
8) a friend in need (   )
9) fed up with (   )
10) lay hands on (   )

Meaning

(a) needing money
(b) including everything; all of it
(c) destroy or damage everything in (an area)
(d) in bed because of illness or injury
(e) henceforth; from now on
(f) obtain; get
(g) remember
(h) unwilling to tolerate any more
(i) try to start again; make a new beginning
(j) a friend who really helps when you need help

96D. Change each of the following sentences with an idiom from Lesson 96C.

1) Nana's been sick in bed with the flu for three days. _____

2) The advancing troops destroyed every village they went through. _____

3) Looters took everything of value from the store. _____

4) Pete, I really need some dough. Could you lend me a twenty? _____

5) Chuck gave me a hand when I needed it. He's a real pal. _____

6) Bunny and Claude had a falling-out, but they're trying to patch things up. _____

7) If I ever catch that kid, if I ever get hold of him, I'll wring his neck. _____

8) I'm sick of your excuses. Either get to work on time, or get another job. _____

9) From now on after this, you have to pay for your own gasoline. _____

10) Remember that you're invited guests here, and conduct yourselves accordingly. _____

The Idiom Book   193

Lesson 97
BANK LOAN

97A. Read.

Jeff: It's a good thing you didn't <u>make a scene</u> at the bank over the interest they want—we really need that loan. We have to do more than just <u>make ends meet</u>, you know; we've got to start <u>making a dent in</u> that pile of bills.

Paul: Yeah, I know, but I just hate to beg for money and then make the bank richer.

Jeff: Look, Paul, our business is right on <u>the main drag</u>. <u>Mark my words</u>: we'll do more than make a killing; we'll <u>make a mint</u>!

Paul: OK, then. Let's <u>go for it</u>.

Jeff: Right on. Let's <u>bite the bullet</u> and get that loan. A year from now, we'll be <u>rolling in dough</u>.

97B. Read and fill in the blanks.

Mary, I want to say something, so just listen for a minute, OK? I'm glad you didn't ___<u>a</u>___ <u>scene</u> at the bank. Sure they're charging us a lot of interest, but remember we have to <u>bite</u> _____ <u>bullet</u> and get this loan in order to <u>make</u> _____ <u>meet</u>. Then we'll be able to start <u>making a</u> _____ in those hospital bills. In fact, we'll do that and more. With the business right on <u>the main</u> _____, we'll _____ <u>a killing</u>. We'll <u>make a</u> _____. We'll be <u>rolling in</u> _____! <u>Mark</u> _____ <u>words</u>: if we don't ___ <u>for it</u> now, we'll never forgive ourselves. Right?

194 The Idiom Book

97C. Matching Exercise. In the parentheses, write the letter of the meaning for each idiom.

Idiom

1) make a scene ( )
2) make ends meet ( )
3) make a dent in ( )
4) the main drag ( )
5) mark my words ( )
6) make a killing ( )
7) rolling in dough ( )
8) bite the bullet ( )
9) go for it ( )
10) make a mint ( )

Meaning

(a) the principal street in a town or city
(b) to reduce the amount or number of something
(c) to have just enough money for essentials
(d) to complain loudly and angrily in public
(e) to try to succeed at, or win, something
(f) do the necessary thing, even if it's difficult or painful
(g) rich; wealthy
(h) to make a huge amount of money
(i) to make a lot of money fast
(j) listen, and remember this:

97D. Change each of the following sentences with an idiom from 97C.

1) Mabel complained loudly and angrily at the post office yesterday about the late mail delivery all week. _____

2) With your mother's help, we'll be able to buy food and pay the rent. _____

3) We have to start to pay some of our debts. _____

4) They always decorate the principal street in our town very prettily at Christmas. _____

5) Listen—she's going to be a problem. _____

6) They made a huge amount of money on real estate in the 90s. _____

7) She made a lot of dough fast on the stock market. _____

8) Cookie, if you really want to be an astronaut, then try! _____

9) I hate to get a new car, but I'm afraid it's time to do it despite the cost. _____

10) If the business succeeds, you'll both be rich. _____

The Idiom Book   195

Lesson 98
COMPANY PROFITS

98A. Read.

Marge: I read the letter from Caspian Gas and I can't <u>make head or tail of</u> it. It's obvious that the writer's <u>mother tongue</u> isn't English.

Nathan: Well, our leader's *is*, and her writing in English <u>leaves much to be desired</u>, too. <u>Many a</u> poor secretary has <u>come to grief</u> trying to <u>make sense of</u> her incoherent paragraphs.

Marge: Yeah. She <u>makes no bones about</u> the fact that she <u>couldn't care less</u> about good writing, but does care passionately about money.

Nathan: That's why she gets paid more than we do. Company profits are for her, as for the firm, <u>the be-all and end-all</u>.

Marge: And <u>needless to say</u>, what she says goes.

98B. Read and fill in the blanks.

Memo

TO: Rob Strout, Purchasing September 13
FROM: Bill Graves, Marketing RE: Language Problems?

Rob, would you take a look at the attached? I can't <u>make</u> or tail of this letter from Kazakhstan. I believe that <u>many</u> company exec is going to <u>come</u> grief trying to <u>make</u> of messages we get from Almaty, because their English <u>leaves much to be</u>. Our <u>mother</u> is Germanic and theirs is Altaic. Translators and interpreters can handle the actual language problems, but the important thing of course is that the cultural differences are much deeper and subtler than the linguistic issues. However, the Kazakhs, and we, <u>couldn't</u> less about cultural sensibilities. <u>The be-</u> and end-all in this process is, for us, getting the gas out to the Black Sea or the Gulf, and for the Kazakhs it's getting paid for what they give us. They <u>make</u> bones about the fact that their concern is money, not cross-cultural communication. <u>Needless</u> <u>say</u>, being insensitive to culture can be dangerous. What do you think?

196 The Idiom Book

98C. Matching Exercise. In the parentheses, write the letter of the meaning for each idiom.

Idiom

1) make head or tail of ( )
2) mother tongue ( )
3) many a ( )
4) leave much to be desired ( )
5) couldn't care less ( )
6) needless to say ( )
7) make no bones about ( )
8) come to grief ( )
9) the be-all and end-all ( )
10) make sense of ( )

Meaning

(a) a lot more than one
(b) to be unsatisfactory; not good enough
(c) one's native language
(d) to understand something
(e) to not care or worry at all (about something)
(f) the most important part of a situation or of a life
(g) obviously; clearly; of course
(h) is open and honest about something
(i) to understand something
(j) to meet defeat or trouble

98D. Change each of the following sentences with an idiom from 98C.

1) I can't understand his "explanation" at all. _____
2) Your first language is usually the one you learn from your mother. _____
3) The amenities in that apartment just aren't good enough. _____
4) A lot more than one student has tried, and failed, to get a higher grade from me. _____
5) The students who flunk this course almost always do so because of laziness. _____
6) I'm trying hard to understand his letter, but the poor chap is almost illiterate. _____
7) She doesn't try to hide her dislike of my choice of restaurants. _____
8) Frankly, my dear, I don't give a damn. _____
9) He's obsessed with her. She's the most important thing in his life. _____
10) And of course I don't have to tell you that these payments must be made on time. _____

Lesson 99
SETTING UP SHOP

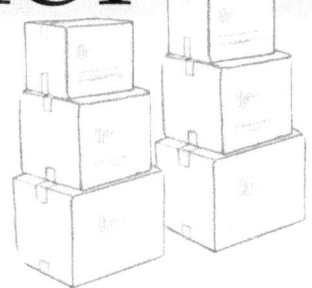

99A. Read.

Levinson: Bartleby, this is your office. Please <u>set up shop</u> here and <u>make yourself at home</u>. There are no <u>hard and fast rules</u>, except this: come to work every day, unless you're sick.

Bartleby: Thanks, JL. I'll <u>keep my nose to the grindstone</u> and should have a proposal for a drama or a sitcom within three weeks, <u>give or take</u>.

Levinson: Splendid. By the way, your work on that documentary was <u>nothing short of</u> brilliant, and we're sure you haven't <u>lost your touch</u>. We're delighted to have you <u>on board</u>.

Bartleby: Thank you. I'll <u>do my best</u> to <u>earn my keep</u> here.

99B. Read and fill in the blanks.

Bosley Frank
Chair, Arts Committee
Hartland, CT 06001

Lydia Erickson
723 Pine Grove Manor
Hartland, CT 06009

Dear Lydia,

    First, thank you so much for your wonderful contribution. You are a true patron of the arts. The new conductor, Leonard Peacock, debuted with Beethoven's Fifth, and it's obvious that he hasn't <u>lost his</u> _____. The performance was <u>nothing</u> _____ <u>of</u> breathtaking. Peacock <u>set up</u> _____ here only four weeks ago, _____ <u>himself at home</u> immediately with both musicians and management, and is <u>keeping everyone's</u> _____ <u>to the grindstone</u>. He has a <u>hard</u> _____ <u>fast</u> rule for everyone: practice, practice, and then practice. He has the orchestra rehearse five hours a day, _____ <u>or take</u>, four days a week. I'm glad he's _____ <u>board</u>; I'm sure he'll <u>earn his</u> _____, and we—the committee—will _____ <u>our best</u> to keep him here.

Best wishes,
Bosley

99C. Matching Exercise. In the parentheses, write the letter of the meaning for each idiom.

Idiom

1) hard and fast ( )
2) make oneself at home ( )
3) set up shop ( )
4) keep one's nose to the grindstone ( )
5) on board ( )
6) do one's best ( )
7) earn one's keep ( )
8) give or take ( )
9) nothing short of ( )
10) lose one's touch ( )

Meaning

(a) to work hard and steadily
(b) definite and unchanging ; invariable
(c) relax and feel comfortable
(d) to start a business or profession
(e) [as] a member of a team
(f) to use all of one's strength or ability; go all out
(g) to do one's share of the work; pull one's weight
(h) to lose the ability to do something well
(i) truly; absolutely
(j) approximately; more or less

99D. Change each of the following sentences with an idiom from 99C.

1) Alfred Wolfson is opening an office in Edinburgh. _____

2) Come in, Mrs. Nye. Please sit down and be comfortable. _____

3) I guess there are no invariable rules in Chinese checkers, for kids, anyway. _____

4) If you don't make her work hard and steadily, she'll never finish. _____

5) From here to Quebec City? Oh, 300 kilometers or so. _____

6) Your writing is absolutely terrible, Cheekley. You're fired. _____

7) He no longer plays the violin well. _____
8) We're very glad you've joined our sales team, Mr. Veter. _____

9) I ran as fast as possible, but I lost the race. _____
10) Thanks for the chance, boss. I'll always do my share. _____

Lesson 100

DEMOTION

100A. Read.

Jane: Phil <u>got used to</u> being <u>the fair-haired boy</u> of this firm, but now he's <u>out of the loop</u> and <u>out of luck</u>.

Erica: Yeah, I heard that the director's nephew replaced him. He was pretty <u>sure of himself</u> before, but that <u>took the wind out of his sails</u>.

Jane: Uh huh. Demotion has a way of doing that to you. <u>Still and all</u>, this is a good place to work because things change here often; and that <u>bodes well for</u> us, since the only way that we can move is up.

Erica: Right. I intend to <u>stay put</u>; I honestly think I might <u>take</u> this place <u>by storm</u> if I'm careful and work hard.

100. Read and fill in the blanks.

Diary

Date: July 27

I <u>was used</u> _____ being pretty <u>sure</u> _____ myself in this job. I was <u>the</u> _____ -haired boy who was sure to <u>take</u> the firm <u>by</u> _____. "Being a favorite of the director," I used to tell myself, "<u>bodes</u> _____ for my chances indeed." But then I was suddenly <u>out</u> _____ the loop, and I still don't know why. Whatever the reason, I'm now _____ of luck. That sure <u>took</u> <u>the</u> _____ out of my sails. <u>Still</u> _____ all, I'll probably be forced to _____ <u>put</u> here, despite the humiliation. How else will I keep body and soul together?

200 The Idiom Book

100C. Matching Exercise. In the parentheses, write the letter of the meaning for each idiom.

Idiom

1) out of the loop ( )
2) the fair-haired boy ( )
3) be/get used to ( )
4) out of luck ( )
5) stay put ( )
6) take the wind out of one's sails ( )
7) bode well for ( )
8) still and all ( )
9) sure of oneself ( )
10) take something by storm ( )

Meaning

(a) prevented from doing or being something that you want
(b) not part of the group that makes decisions or gets important information
(c) a person that someone in authority likes and favors
(d) be/get accustomed to
(e) is a sign that the future will be good
(f) not move; not go away
(g) to be very successful at something
(h) nonetheless
(i) to suddenly make someone feel less confident
(j) self-confident

100D. Change each of the following sentences with an idiom from 100C.

1) I was quite accustomed to living in a small town. _____

2) That guy is the boss's favorite trainee. He'll do well here. _____

3) I'm no longer one of the group that's kept informed and makes decisions. _____

4) Sorry—you can't get to Springfield tonight: the railroad's on strike. _____

5) I was cocky—too self-confident—and I lost the race. _____

6) Losing the race suddenly made me feel much less confident. _____

7) The ice is only about four centimeters thick. Even so, I'm going to skate. _____

8) We got the contract for the school year. That makes things look pretty good, at least for the near future. _____

9) Now kids, don't move while I take these pictures. _____

10) Stella Stunning was a huge success in her very first Hollywood picture. _____

The Idiom Book 201

Lesson 101
SOONER OR LATER

101A. Read.

Pedro: John! You're <u>a sight for sore eyes</u>. How've you been?

John: <u>Ah, same old, same old</u>. And you?

Pedro: Pretty good, really. I'm <u>on a roll</u> with my business and I'm finally <u>in the black</u>.

John: I knew you'd <u>make good</u>—<u>sooner or later</u>.

Pedro: You mean "<u>better late than never</u>," or "<u>I had my doubts</u>?"

John: Sorry. I suppose that sounded snide, but I didn't mean it to. I think it's wonderful.

Pedro: No—<u>I'm sorry</u>. I didn't mean to <u>snap your head off</u>. Say, let's not <u>lose track of</u> each other again.

John: Right. This time, we'll have to keep <u>in touch</u>.

101B. Read and fill in the blanks.

JOURNAL ENTRY FOR: 10/15, on the road to Saskatoon—I hope.

After we'd driven 170 miles, that service area was a <u>sight for sore ____</u>. The meal we got wasn't great, but when you're hungry, you can only say to yourself, <u>better late ____ never</u> when you finally find a place to eat. Our family business is <u>on ____ roll</u>, we're <u>in the ____</u> again (I think we've <u>____ good</u>), and Fred and I like to drive out through the North American prairie and get <u>____ touch</u> with old friends we <u>lost ____</u> of through the years. We stopped to see Marilyn. She's always the same. In fact, she always says, "<u>same old, ____ old</u>" when we meet. When we left Bismarck, I told Fred we were going the wrong way. Of course, he <u>snapped my ____ off</u> when I suggested that he may have got us lost. So anyway, the motel here in Billings isn't bad, and I console myself with the thought that, <u>sooner ____ later</u>, we'll find the road to Saskatoon.

202 The Idiom Book

101C. Matching Exercise. In the parentheses write the letter of the meaning for each idiom.

Idiom

1) sight for sore eyes ( )
2) same old, same old ( )
3) in the black ( )
4) on a roll ( )
5) lose track of ( )
6) sooner or later ( )
7) snap someone's head off ( )
8) better late than never ( )
9) make good ( )
10) in touch ( )

Meaning

(a) not financially in debt
(b) quite successful, at least temporarily
(c) OK, but not great
(d) someone or something you're very glad to see
(e) to speak harshly and angrily to someone
(f) to no longer know where someone is
(g) in communication
(h) doing something worthwhile late is better than not doing it at all
(i) eventually
(j) to succeed professionally

101D. Change each of the following sentences with an idiom from 101C.

1) Billy! I'm so glad to see you! _____
2) "How was Justin?" "Oh, not bad." _____
3) Deal those cards—I can't lose! _____
4) Business has improved a lot. I'm finally out of debt. _____
   _____
5) In fact, I think I can say I've succeeded, financially. _____
   _____
6) Someday she'll stop rambling. I hope. _____
7) Even if it takes you, say, six years to finish college, it's still better than not going. _____
   _____
8) Hey, damn it. There's no need to speak to me like that. _____
   _____
9) She was my best friend, and now I don't know where she lives. _____
   _____
10) Make sure to send me your new address and phone number. _____
    _____

The Idiom Book 203

Other Books from Pro Lingua for Intermediate/Advanced Learners

All Around America: The Time Traveler's Talk Show. The show stops at 18 famous places around the US. Learners read the script which includes a host, a local guide, guests from the past, and callers from the present. Supplemented with an Activities Workbook that builds language skills, with emphasis on idiomatic spoken language. All the scripts are also recorded on two **CDs** for listening practice.

Dictations for Discussion. Over 50 dictation lessons in four different formats—partial dictation, paired dictations, dictogloss, and prediction. The dictation texts feature six different topical areas: cultural trends, money and work, holidays/special events, ethics, health, and language facts and fun. Two **CDs** are available. A **digital edition** with audio is also available.

Lexicarry. A vocabulary builder that also stimulates speaking and listening skills. 4500 unlabeled pictures with an English key in the index. Pictures are arranged in categories: Functions, Sequences, Related Actions, Operations, Topics, Places, Proverbs, and Sayings. Additional WORD LISTS are available in Spanish, French, Italian, Brazilian Portuguese, German, Japanese, Chinese, Korean, Mongolian, Hungarian, and Turkish.

The Modal Book. Fourteen units explore the form, meaning, and use of the American English modal verb system, one semantic grouping at a time. Each unit also explores the sights and sounds of a different country, from Brazil to Turkey.

A Phrasal Verb Affair. When John runs out on Maria and runs off with another woman, Maria tracks him down to do him in. 15 dramatic episodes in the style of a soap opera introduce the learners to over 200 phrasal verbs. Lots of exercises. The text is accompanied by a dramatization of the script on a **CD**. A **digital edition** with audio is also available.

Writing Strategies. Two texts jam-packed with writing activities. Each covers four modes of writing. **Book One (high-intermediate)** teaches description, narration, exposition, comparison and contrast, and expository essay with a source. **Book Two (advanced)** covers process, cause and effect, extended definition, argumentation, and essay with a source and mixed mode essay. Coordinated with these lessons are fluency writing exercises and lessons on grammar problems and terminology. **Write After Input.** Low-intermediate. Focused on writing good paragraphs.

Pro Lingua Learning
PO Box 4467
Rockville, MD 20849 USA

Orders: (800) 888-4741
Inqueries/Advice Hotline: (301) 424-8900
Email: info@ProLinguaLearning.com
Web: www.ProLinguaLearning.com

Questions? Simply give us a call and we'll try to help.

www.ingramcontent.com/pod-product-compliance
Lightning Source LLC
Chambersburg PA
CBHW080432230426
43662CB00015B/2250